636.72 POO

• DOG BREED HANDBOOKS •
POODLE

• Dog Breed Handbooks •
POODLE

DR. BRUCE FOGLE

SPECIAL PHOTOGRAPHY BY
TRACY MORGAN

DORLING KINDERSLEY
LONDON · NEW YORK · STUTTGART · MOSCOW

A DORLING KINDERSLEY BOOK

Project Editor NIC KYNASTON
Art Editor STEFAN MORRIS
Editor KAREN O'BRIEN
Designer CLARE DRISCOLL
Managing Editor FRANCIS RITTER
Managing Art Editor DEREK COOMBES
DTP Designer SONIA CHARBONNIER
Picture Researcher MELISSA ALBANY
Production Controller RUTH CHARLTON

First published in Great Britain in 1997
by Dorling Kindersley Limited,
9 Henrietta Street, London WC2E 8PS

Visit us on the World Wide Web at
http://www.dk.com

A CIP catalogue record for this book is
available from the British Library

ISBN 0 7513 03097

Reproduced by Colourpath, London
Printed and bound in Italy by Graphicom

CONTENTS

INTRODUCTION

W̶E LIKE TO THINK that humans domesticated the dog, but this is only partly true. Although the dog has been our partner for longer than any other species of animal, we did not actively domesticate it. Over 12,000 years ago, our ancestors in Asia founded permanent settlements. Local Asiatic wolves – sociable by nature – were attracted to these locations and moved into surrounding areas to scavenge for

It seems difficult to believe that the wolf is a relative, albeit a distant one, of the gentle, affectionate Poodle

food. As natural food was scarce, only the smallest and tamest of these wolves survived in their new environment. Early human settlers recognized the potential of these creatures, captured "wolf-dog" puppies, and raised them for guarding and hunting.

ADAPTATION OF THE BREEDS
By 6,000 years ago, selective breeding by humans had produced dogs with most of the characteristics that exist today. Hunting dogs that followed scent trails and retrieved game, and smaller companion dogs, were present in Europe at least 1,000 years ago. By the

This 19th-century illustration shows the popularity of the water-loving Poodle as a ship's dog

Middle Ages, hunters in Europe had selectively bred dogs with thick, waterproof coats that could cope with waterlogged, marshy terrain, as well as retrieve game from rivers and lakes. These "Water Dogges", as they were then known in Britain, were later to be called Poodles, taken from the German verb "*pudeln*", meaning to splash around in water.

Swimming was made easier for the Poodle by clipping its coat; pompoms insulated body parts from the cold water

SENSIBLE, POPULAR, AND VERSATILE

Careful breeding down the centuries has created three distinct sizes of Poodle – Standard, Miniature, and Toy. Poodles can thus fulfil a variety of roles – from small companion dogs that are ideally suited to urban environments, to large working dogs that can quickly learn skills

The Poodle is a gregarious dog that responds well to all kinds of training

as diverse as scent trailing, obedience, and agility. Poodles and Poodle crossbreeds, such as the Labradoodle, are sometimes used to fulfil a range of assistance roles, from sniffer dogs at airports to guide dogs for the blind. The breed's discerning, responsive, fun-loving qualities have all contributed to giving the Poodle its unique place in the canine world.

The Labradoodle, a Labrador-Poodle cross, is an excellent guide dog for blind people

GLAMOROUS AND GRACEFUL

The Poodle's unique coat, which never moults, can be clipped into a multitude of different styles, from the striking lion or English saddle trim, with its unusual pompoms on the ankles and tail, to the short, practical lamb trim, ideal for pets and working dogs. The Poodle's graceful movement, combined with its aristocratic looks and gentle personality, made it one of the most widely owned dogs of the 20th century.

From small Toys to giant Standards, Poodles display one of the largest size ranges of any dog breed

THE IDEAL CHOICE

THERE ARE FEW BREEDS of dog that range in size as much as the Poodle. All sizes, whether Standard, Miniature, or Toy, share common looks and coat colours, but each type has some variation in needs and personality. Small dogs make ideal urban pets, while larger Poodles require a great deal more living space.

LONGEVITY AND EXCELLENT HEALTH

Poodles can be expected to live longer than most other breeds of dog. Standard Poodles can live up to 17 years, while Miniatures and Toys often reach 14 or 15 years. Often they maintain their playfulness and physical dexterity well into their senior years. Poodles are generally hardy, extremely responsive, and, if cared for properly, should lead very long lives. Compared with most other breeds, Poodles have a lower than average incidence of skin disorders. Because Poodles do not moult, they can make excellent pets for people who have certain allergies.

Older Poodle still retains its urge to play

GREAT AND SMALL

Toy and Miniature Poodles make ideal pets in urban environments, and are easy to transport for holidays and weekend trips. Standard Poodles need more space, and require ample room in your vehicle during journeys. Also consider the maintenance and feeding costs of the different sizes.

A LOYAL PROTECTOR

While a Standard Poodle may look formidable, it is not a natural barker. Miniatures and Toys, on the other hand, willingly alert their owners to the slightest disturbance outside the home, and make very effective guard dogs. Control your Poodle's barking by training it when it is still a puppy.

Standard Poodle has been trained to bark on command

GROOMING REQUIREMENTS

While the Poodle's coat is one of its most attractive attributes, it does require regular care. Traditional clipping often reduces the time owners need to spend on grooming. All coats need frequent attention to prevent the hairs from matting. Maintaining the coat requires either your time or paying for professional grooming.

Adult dog relaxes for routine grooming

NATURAL LOVE OF WATER

Poodles love splashing about in water; they were originally bred as sporting dogs, and were used to retrieve fowl, often from rivers and streams. Standard Poodles, in particular, are excellent swimmers, and are protected in cold waters by their profuse, dense coats. If you take your Poodle for a walk in the countryside, or near to water, be prepared to clean a muddy, wet coat afterwards!

AN AFFABLE FAMILY COMPANION

All Poodles, whether Standard, Miniature, or Toy, love being members of the family; the Poodle is a breed that needs daily mental as well as physical stimulation. Poodles of all sizes are delightful to have as members of the household; their vivacious personality means that they are particularly popular with children, and they make precocious, responsive pets. It is no accident that Poodles were once circus dogs – their ability to stand on their hind legs and to master any number of obedience tasks makes them rewarding pets.

Miniature Poodle is a well-loved part of the family

THE STANDARD POODLE

THE IMPRESSIVE STANDARD Poodle is the largest of the three Poodle sizes. In most countries, any Poodle that is larger than 38 cm (15 in) in height is classified as a Standard-sized dog, although they can grow even bigger. The Standard Poodle's alert, discriminating nature and gentle character make it one of the most rewarding of all large dogs.

COLOUR
All solid colours. Whites and creams have black nose, lips, and eye rims

TAIL
Set on high, carried at slight angle away from body, never curled

FOREQUARTERS
Shoulders well laid back, strong, and muscular

HINDQUARTERS
Thighs well developed and muscular. Hind legs turning neither in nor out

COAT
Very profuse and dense; of harsh texture. Short hair is close, thick, and curly

FEET
Tight, proportionally small, oval in shape

A UNIQUE COAT

The Poodle's coat is one of its many fascinating features. Almost unique among dog coats in that it never stops growing, it can be clipped into a variety of styles. This feature also means that the Poodle can make an ideal pet for people who have an allergy to moulted dog hair.

KEEN SENSES AND AN ASTUTE DISPOSITION
Poodles have excellent eyesight and a sharp sense
of smell, which has led to their use as scenting
hounds. The Standard Poodle's bright sensibility
and gentle nature mean that it responds very
effectively to obedience and agility training.

EYES
*Almond-
shaped, full
of fire and
intelligence*

POODLE SIZES

Although the Standard Poodle is the oldest
size of the breed, records from as far back as
1792 show that the Poodle was bred in two
distinct sizes. However, it was not until 1911
that the Miniature size was recognized as a
separate category by the Kennel Club of
Great Britain. The smallest size of Poodle, the
Toy, was not officially classified as a distinct
size in Great Britain until 1957. In some
countries, an intermediate classification
between the Miniature and the Standard
Poodle, called a Medium, is also allowed.

A GRACEFUL, ELEGANT COMPANION
The Standard Poodle moves with a
light, elegant grace that is due to its
well-balanced, evenly proportioned
body, its strong forequarters, and its
well-developed, muscular thighs. The
Poodle's proud carriage belies a
good-tempered constitution, a playful
nature, and an extrovert personality.

HEAD AND SKULL
*Head in proportion
to size of dog. Skull
not broad; cheekbones
and muscle flat*

EARS
*Leathers long
and wide, set
low, hanging
close to face*

MEASUREMENTS (BRITISH BREED STANDARD)
STANDARD POODLE

Height (at shoulder):
Over 38 cm (15 in)
There is no separate height
stipulated for males or females

1.8 m
(6 ft)

THE MINIATURE POODLE

THE MINIATURE POODLE is a compact, easily trained dog with a gentle nature, and is ranked between the Standard and the Toy Poodles in size. This variety first became popular at the beginning of the 20th century, when breeders saw the potential of a dog that retained the Standard Poodle's grace and beauty, but in a smaller, more manageable size.

GENTLE, ENTERTAINING SHOW-OFFS

Poodles love being the centre of attention, and thrive on human company. They are gentle dogs and seldom experience aggression-related problems. The Miniature Poodle in particular can be very playful around children.

BACK AND LOINS
Back short, strong, and slightly hollowed; loins broad and muscular

HEAD AND SKULL
Foreface well chiselled, not falling away under eyes. Lips tight-fitting

MOVEMENT
Should be sound, free, and light, with lots of drive

THE RISE OF THE MINIATURE

There has long been a large range of sizes in the Poodle breed, but it was only in 1911 that the Miniature variety was recognized by the Kennel Club of Great Britain. However, the Miniature Poodle became a victim of its own success; in the mid-1950s, these dogs were one of the most popular varieties worldwide, and some unscrupulous breeders produced inferior dogs to meet the demand. The Miniature's popularity waned, leaving professional breeders to repair the damage. Today, however, the standard of pedigree Miniature Poodles is once again impressive.

A VERSATILE PET AND WORKING DOG
Although classed as a Utility rather than a Working dog, the Poodle can nevertheless make an excellent gun dog. The Miniature Poodle's size makes it adept at going under bushes to flush out the most obstinate game, and its fearless character and boundless energy enable it to pursue most quarry.

COLOUR
Blacks, silvers, and blues have black nose, lips, eye rims, and toenails

NECK
Strong, to allow head to be carried high and with dignity

FOREQUARTERS
Legs set straight back from shoulders, well muscled

STYLISH AND SOPHISTICATED
Not only does the Poodle sometimes affect a regal, almost haughty attitude, but its appearance firmly places it within the realms of the fascinating and the fashionable. Its strong, curly coat that never sheds gives a unique, instantly recognizable appearance.

MEASUREMENTS (BRITISH BREED STANDARD)
MINIATURE POODLE
Height (at shoulder):
Under 38 cm (15 in) but
not under 28 cm (11 in)
There is no separate height
stipulated for males or females

1.8 m
(6 ft)

THE TOY POODLE

THE MOST RECENT size category to be classified in the Poodle breed, the Toy Poodle is one of the world's most popular dogs. Despite the Toy's small stature, it retains the vitality, exuberance, and energy of the larger members of the breed. Toy dogs make practical, rewarding companions in urban environments, where space may be limited.

AN AGILE, ENERGETIC ACROBAT
The Toy Poodle is a dynamic ball of energy, and relishes exercise. Its agility and fun-loving nature are epitomized by the fact that many Toys love jumping up, or even walking, on their hind legs.

TAIL
Thick at root; often docked, though not now necessary for show ring

COLOUR
Silvers, apricots, browns, creams, and blues may show varying shades of the same colour up to the age of 18 months

COAT
Usually trimmed regularly, unless corded coat is desired

TOES
Toes arched; pads are thick, hard, and well cushioned

DEVOTED, HARDY DOGS

Toy Poodles make very loyal pets. In spite of their small size, they are fearless and will vocally defend their owner's property. Although it might be assumed that such small dogs do not have a robust constitution, Toy Poodles are actually hardy dogs and often live for up to 15 years.

HEAD AND SKULL
Long and fine with slight peak. Chin well defined, but not protruding

MOUTH
Jaws strong with perfect, regular, complete scissor bite

NECK
Well proportioned, and long. Skin fits tightly at throat

TOY POODLE ORIGINS

Although the precise origins of the Toy Poodle are debatable, very small Poodles were firmly established by the end of the 18th century, and were very popular as lap-dogs for women of the aristocracy. Attempts have been made to link the Toy's genealogy to many other breeds of dog, including the Spaniel, the Terrier, the Maltese, and the Havanese. However, breeders developed the modern-day Toy Poodle by selectively mating small Miniature dogs with each other. This size category of Poodle was only first recognized by kennel and breed clubs around the world in the 1940s and 1950s.

A PLAYFUL, AFFECTIONATE COMPANION

Miniaturization sometimes brings with it a heightened, puppy-like dependency on people. However, the Toy Poodle has retained the independent personality of larger Poodles, and is an energetic and delightful companion.

MEASUREMENTS (BRITISH BREED STANDARD) TOY POODLE

Height (at shoulder):
Under 28 cm (11 in)
There is no separate height
stipulated for males or females

1.8 m
(6 ft)

BEHAVIOUR PROFILE

EVERY DOG'S PERSONALITY is shaped in part by its experiences within the litter, and later with you. Heredity is also important, and selective breeding has given each size of Poodle a distinctive behaviour profile. Overall, the breed's responsiveness and friendly disposition have made it a worldwide favourite.

TRAINABILITY/OBEDIENCE

Standard Poodles, like other dogs originally bred to work, are highly trainable. Miniatures also rate above average, similar to the English Springer Spaniel or American Cocker Spaniel. Toy Poodles are more difficult to obedience-train, on a par with Beagles and Akitas.

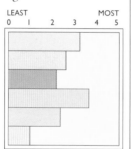

PLAYFULNESS WITH OTHER DOGS

Similar to Boxers and Irish Setters, Standard Poodles are among the most playful of dogs. Miniatures are just above average in their willingness to play with other dogs, while Toy Poodles are much less enthusiastic, not unlike the Finnish Spitz and Corgi.

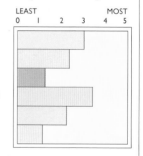

BARKING TO PROTECT THE HOME

Although Standard Poodles have formidable physical presence, they are not renowned for barking to warn of potential intruders. Miniatures are far more vocal, above average, while Toys are even better as household sentries, ranking alongside the Dachshund.

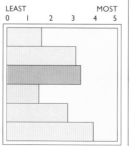

EXCITABILITY

Generally, Poodles are not the most placid of breeds. However, Standard and Miniature types are only slightly more excitable than the average dog. Toys rate significantly higher for this characteristic, although Irish Setters vie with them for top ranking.

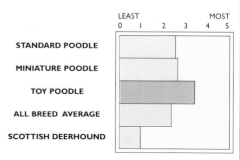

HOW TO USE THE BEHAVIOUR CHARTS

In a recent study, vets and dog breeders assessed over 100 breeds, rating each on a scale of 0–5 for specific personality traits, with 0 representing the lowest score among all dogs and 5 the highest. Here, for eight different behaviours, Standard, Miniature, and Toy Poodles are compared with the statistically "average" canine, as well as with breeds rated at both extremes for each characteristic. Note that the findings do not take the dog's sex or coat colour into consideration, and apply to the breed as a whole, not to individuals.

RELIABLE WITH STRANGE CHILDREN

Surprisingly for such a small dog, the Toy Poodle is under-average in its reliability with unknown children. Miniatures are rather steadier, while Standards are more reliable than most breeds. Monitor meetings between your Poodle and new children.

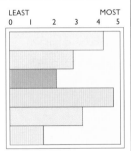

LEAST 0 1 2 3 MOST 4 5

STANDARD POODLE
MINIATURE POODLE
TOY POODLE
NEWFOUNDLAND
ALL BREED AVERAGE
CHOW CHOW

CALM IN NEW CIRCUMSTANCES

Like the easy-going Labrador, Standard Poodles tend to take strange situations in their stride. Miniatures are less calm than average, while Toy Poodles are more liable to react nervously, although the Miniature Pinscher outdoes them in this quality.

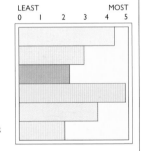

LEAST 0 1 2 3 MOST 4 5

STANDARD POODLE
MINIATURE POODLE
TOY POODLE
NEWFOUNDLAND
ALL BREED AVERAGE
MINIATURE PINSCHER

DESTRUCTIVE WHEN ALONE

Some dogs, when left alone at home, can damage items out of boredom or anxiety. However, Standard and Miniature Poodles rank well below average for destructiveness, and Toys are no worse than average, similar to Lhasa Apsos and Scandinavian Drevers.

LEAST 0 1 2 3 MOST 4 5

STANDARD POODLE
MINIATURE POODLE
TOY POODLE
NEWFOUNDLAND
ALL BREED AVERAGE
DOBERMAN

HOUSE TRAINABLE

Virtually all dogs respond well to house training, and Poodles cover the entire range. Toys tie with Yorkshire Terriers as the most difficult breed to house-train, Miniatures are exactly average, while Standards rank at the top, with Labradors and German Shepherds.

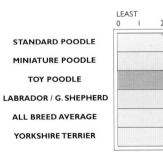

LEAST 0 1 2 3 MOST 4 5

STANDARD POODLE
MINIATURE POODLE
TOY POODLE
LABRADOR / G. SHEPHERD
ALL BREED AVERAGE
YORKSHIRE TERRIER

COATS AND COLOURS

THE UNIQUE COAT of the Poodle is one of its most appealing features. The thick, curly hair appears in a range of solid colours, from black to white, with many colours in between. Parti-coloured Poodles, dogs with two distinct colours in the coat, are becoming more popular, though they are not officially recognized.

COAT-COLOUR HISTORY

Poodles' coats appear in a spectrum of solid colours. The most commonly seen are black and white, but there is a wide range of shades in between, including blue, silver, apricot, brown, red, and cream. In recent times, the official breed standard has specified that Poodles should have coats of a solid colour; two-coloured dogs, known as parti-colours, are allowed only as pets, and are disqualified from the show ring by the breed standard. However, paintings from the 17th to the 19th centuries show that parti-coloured Poodles were once extremely popular.

SHADES OF CREAM
Cream, and a slightly darker shade known as apricot, are among the most attractive of Poodle coat colours. At birth, these Poodles often have much darker coats, usually shaded red.

WHITE COATS
A Poodle with a white coat looks stunning, but potential owners should remember that the slightest speck of dirt will make it appear dirty, and that it consequently requires more grooming than a darker dog. Poodles with white coats should have dark pigmentation in their eye rims, lips, and nails.

SILVER COATS
Silver Poodles (and their grey relations) are usually born a very dark, almost black, colour. It generally takes around 18 months for the distinctive silver tone to develop fully throughout their coats.

PARTI-COLOURED POODLES

Although the Poodle breed standard does not allow parti-coloured Poodles in the show ring, they nevertheless make attractive pets. These dogs are becoming ever more popular in parts of Europe and the United States, where black-and-white dogs, sometimes known as harlequin Poodles, have been produced, as well as black-and-tan dogs with markings similar to those of a Doberman Pinscher or a Rottweiler. Breeders have also recently produced a brindle coat, which is a mixture of black hairs and lighter-colour hairs spread throughout the coat. The parti-coloured Poodle looks set to become a sought-after variety.

CORDED POODLES

There is debate as to whether the Corded Poodle should be classified as a distinct type of Poodle, or simply as an "ordinary" Poodle whose coat has been left uncut and trained into long cords. The popularity of the Corded Poodle reached its peak at the turn of the 20th century; now, this type of coat is seldom seen.

BROWNS AND REDS

Poodle coats appear in a wide range of shades of brown – from rich chocolate through to the most recent official colour, red, as well as a lighter variant that is sometimes called *café au lait*. Brown Poodles should always have amber eyes and liver-coloured noses and foot pads.

BLACK AND BLUE COATS

At first sight, many so-called blue Poodles seem to be black. However, in bright sunlight, or when contrasted with a dog with a black coat, the blue's unusual colouring is apparent. Here, the dog lying down has a blue coat, while the dog sitting to the right of it has a black coat.

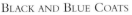

PIGMENT AND PERSONALITY

SURVEYS COMPLETED BY Poodle breeders report on the link
between coat colour and temperament. This link is probably
the colour pigment melanin, which is similar to chemicals that
act as transmitters in the brain. The Poodle's personality is also
influenced by size, breeding line, and early learning experiences.

RESULTS OF THE SURVEYS

AN ACTIVE AND PLAYFUL BREED

Poodles are more active and playful, and less
aggressive than most dogs. The Poodle appears
in a wide range of solid coat colours, and
variants of those colours. Although breeders
are not always in agreement as to the link
between a Poodle's personality and its specific
coat colour, the results of the surveys indicate
some basic behavioural differences.

*Blue Poodle (far right)
is similar to black one
(right) in personality
and temperament*

*Apricot Poodles
sometimes need
coaxing to play*

COAT COLOUR AND BEHAVIOUR

Breeders reported no significant differences
related to coat colour in the following areas
of Poodle behaviour: protective or anxious
barking, enjoyment at being petted, excitability,
aggressiveness to strangers entering the home,
or likelihood of snapping at unknown
children. However, coat colour was found to
influence other behavioural patterns. Black
Poodles were reported to be more obedient
and easier to house-train than Poodles with
other coat colours, while apricots were
found to be more likely to be
disobedient and more difficult
to house-train than average.

COLOUR-RELATED DIFFERENCES

Breeders of Standard Poodles were asked to complete a survey about a variety of Poodle behaviours according to coat colour. The general trends that were revealed also apply, to a lesser degree, to Miniatures and Toys. The lowest possible score is 0 and the highest is 5. These results can serve only as general guidance and cannot be applied categorically to individual Poodles of any type.

PLAYFULNESS WITH OTHER DOGS

The survey shows that black Poodles are most willing to play with other dogs. Whites are also more playful than average. Apricots and browns are less likely to initiate play.

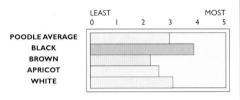

TRAINABILITY/OBEDIENCE

Black Standards are better than average at responding to obedience training. Browns and whites are average for the breed, while apricots require a little more patience.

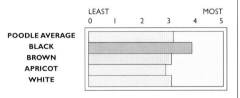

WARINESS OF UNKNOWN PEOPLE

Black and brown Standards are most at ease when meeting unknown people. Whites are typical of the Poodle average, while apricots are a little less sure of themselves.

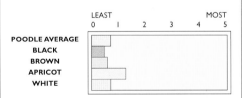

WHINING FOR ATTENTION

Standard Poodles seldom whine for attention, but, within the breed, blacks are least likely to moan or grizzle. Apricots are most likely to make noise to gain attention.

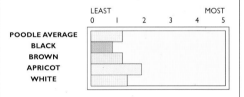

DESTRUCTIVENESS AT HOME

Poodles are less destructive at home than almost any other breed. Within the breed, blacks are least likely to chew furniture; browns and apricots are the most likely.

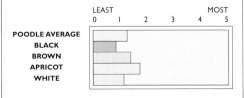

NEED FOR PHYSICAL ACTIVITY

All Poodles thrive on physical activity. However, apricot and white Standards demand slightly less activity than average, while blacks require more physical exercise.

SEX AND TYPE DIFFERENCES

POODLES EXHIBIT FEWER pronounced sex-related differences in behaviour than many other breeds. The greatest difference in the appearance of Poodles is in their trims. Some clips are time-consuming and need professional stylists, while others are more practical and are easier to maintain.

PHYSIQUE AND TEMPERAMENT: THE SEXES COMPARED

Male Poodles are only marginally larger than females, and are similar to females in looks. There are virtually no differences between the sexes in protective barking, the need to be petted, excitability, disobedience, nervousness, or need for physical activity.

Females respond well to house and obedience training

ACTIVE, RESPONSIVE FEMALE

Female Poodles are considered easier to train, and are less likely to be destructive than male Poodles. Neutering has little effect on their personality profile; they remain affable and inquisitive dogs. Female Toy Poodles can be more anxious than male Toys in the presence of strange children.

GENDER-SPECIFIC MEDICAL PROBLEMS

A variety of diseases are caused or influenced by sex hormones. Unless they are spayed early in life, females of all breeds may suffer from mammary tumours (breast cancer) and pyometra (womb infection). Uncastrated males sometimes develop perianal tumours, testicular cancer, or prostate disorders, with associated pain or bleeding during urination. Neutering is part of the preferred treatment for all gender-related medical conditions, but it must be followed by diet control to prevent potential weight gain.

ASSURED MALE

Male Poodles can be more assertive than females, and are more likely to be dominant with other dogs. Males are more wary of strangers approaching their homes, although there is virtually no difference between the sexes in protective barking. Male Poodles demand slightly more physical activity, and are moderately less excitable than females.

Show or Practical Clip?

Clipped for the Show Ring

Breed standards require that Poodles must be shown only in specific trims. The continental trim and the traditional lion clip – called the English saddle clip in the United States – are the most common, although recently other trims have been accepted. The respective trims are appropriate for separate classes of entry in shows. These trims give Poodles a distinctive appearance and, by shaping them in such detail, display their impressive form and stature. Show trims need routine maintenance from experienced groomers.

Poodle displays correct show-ring deportment

Standard brown in lamb trim – a popular, practical style

This Standard white is clipped in the show-ring style known as the second puppy trim

Practical Clipping

Most pet Poodles are kept in simple trims that are easy to maintain. Puppies are clipped only on the face, feet, and tail. When the coat is scissored into shape, it can be in the style of the lamb or sporting trims, both of which are practical cuts throughout a Poodle's life. Trims are needed every 8-10 weeks. In hot weather, the lamb trim is often cut close to the skin to create the town-and-country clip.

Effects of Neutering on Temperament

Some dogs are neutered as a means of population control, while others are neutered for behavioural problems. Although male Poodles rarely need to be neutered for aggressiveness, male Toys and Miniatures are sometimes neutered to overcome indoor urine marking behaviour. In some cases, neutering can make a naturally dominant bitch even more dominant.

THE RIGHT START

BEFORE DECIDING TO ACQUIRE a Poodle, consider how a dog would fit in with your lifestyle. Seek expert advice so that you can make an informed, responsible choice. Be sure to view several litters before selecting a puppy, then prepare your home for the new arrival to ensure a smooth introduction for all.

WHERE TO BUY AND WHAT TO LOOK FOR

CONSULT A VETERINARIAN

Vets and their staff are an excellent source of free, unbiased advice on what to look for in a healthy Poodle. They are aware of any prevalent medical problems and behavioural idiosyncracies. Local dog training clubs may also be able to recommend specific breeders.

ANIMAL RESCUE CENTRES

Dog shelters and rescue societies occasionally have adult Poodles in need of new homes. These dogs can make devoted companions and have usually either been lost or given up for economic reasons, rather than discarded because of behavioural problems.

DECIDING ON THE AGE AND SIZE

Firstly, decide on what size of Poodle fits your home and budget – Standards require a lot of feeding! Then you must choose the age of your new companion. Puppies are very appealing, and acquiring a young dog gives you the opportunity to mould its behaviour to suit your daily routine. Be prepared, however, to invest a lot of time and energy in initial training. If this is too daunting, consider obtaining a trained adult Poodle, but find out as much as you can about its personality. If you are new to the breed, ask other owners about their Poodles.

Choose puppy that is neither too bold nor overly shy

SETTLING IN AT HOME

ARRIVING HOME

Your new puppy is likely to feel disorientated when it arrives in your home. Initially restrict it to just one room with an impervious floor, and introduce it to its own secure "den", preferably a grilled dog crate. Lay soft bedding in one section and an equal area of clean newspaper for toileting. Make the crate inviting by placing food, water, and a chewable toy inside, and leave the door open.

FIRST NIGHT ALONE

Your puppy's first night away from its mother is the hardest, but it should settle down eventually and sleep. If you prefer, you can take your puppy's crate into your bedroom, so that you can keep an eye on it. After it has sufficiently rested, bring in any other pets you may have. Keep the puppy's crate door closed so that you can control their first meetings.

HEALTH CHECKS FOR YOUR NEW DOG

Vet performs full health check

Make any purchase conditional upon your vet's confirmation that the dog is healthy, with no sign of infectious disease, parasites, or malnutrition. The breeder should provide you with documents verifying that a puppy's parents are free from a variety of hereditary disorders. By law, if a puppy is not healthy at the time of sale, the buyer is entitled to a refund or a replacement.

MEET THE PARENTS

Responsible breeders, both amateur and professional, are proud of their stock and will be delighted to introduce you to the litter's mother and also the father, if available. The parents' appearance and behaviour will give you an idea of your puppy's mature size and likely temperament. Be cautious with individuals who are unable to show you the puppy's mother; they may be acting as agents for puppy farms, where Poodles are bred purely for profit, often in uncaring, unsanitary conditions. Also be wary of all but the very best pet shops; some buy from puppy mills.

EARLY TRAINING

POODLES ARE EXCELLENT learners, and respond willingly to rewards such as praise, petting, food treats, and stimulating toys. Start gentle obedience and house training as soon as you bring your puppy home, and arrange regular contact with other dogs to ensure proper social development.

LEARNING WITH REWARDS

VERBAL PRAISE
Poodles are enthusiastic pupils; be just as enthusiastic when giving commands to your puppy. Even eight-week-old puppies understand when you are genuinely pleased with their behaviour. Positive words of praise should always accompany any food or petting rewards.

Stroke chest or side rather than head

Puppy knows it has done well when it hears "Good dog!"

STROKING REWARD
Physical contact is a very powerful reward for your puppy. Your Poodle will naturally want to be stroked, but do not comply on demand. Instead, give a gentle command, then reward obedience with petting.

FOOD TREAT
Standard Poodles usually respond well to food rewards, but Miniatures and Toys are often less interested. Experiment with different snacks to discover which your puppy likes most, then use these, combined with praise, to reward good behaviour.

Puppy receives favourite food as reward

ACQUIRING SOCIAL SKILLS

A puppy's ability to learn is at its greatest during the first three months of life. If denied routine contact with other dogs during this important stage, your Poodle may not develop the social skills necessary for meeting strange dogs later in life. If you do not have another dog, ask your vet to recommend or even help you to organize regular, supervised "puppy parties" to encourage natural, friendly interaction between puppies of a similar age. When walking your puppy, try to avoid aggressive-looking dogs; confrontation can be traumatic for your pet.

Toys for your New Puppy

Suitable Toys for Chewing and Playing

Most Poodles enjoy playing with toys, especially squeaky ones. Keep a maximum of four toys that are fun to chase, retrieve, capture, and chew, or that have a distinctive odour. Teach your puppy that toys belong to you by letting it see you put all items away after play. This discourages possessiveness and demonstrates that you are in charge.

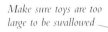

Make sure toys are too large to be swallowed

Toy is offered sparingly, in response to good behaviour

Toys as Reward and Comfort

While toys left lying around soon become boring, items brought out only under special circumstances make exciting rewards. If given selectively as a prize for good behaviour, toys can be highly effective training aids. When you leave your puppy alone, provide it with a toy for comforting distraction.

House Training Indoors and Out

Paper Training

Your puppy will usually want to eliminate after waking, eating, drinking, or exercise. It may signal this by putting its nose down and sniffing. Quickly place the dog in an area covered with newspaper, then praise it when it eliminates. It is pointless to punish your puppy after an accident. If you catch it in the act in the wrong place, sternly say "No!" and take it to the paper or outside.

Moving Outside

Start outdoor training as soon as possible. A three-month-old Poodle needs to empty its bladder about once every three hours. Take a small piece of soiled paper with you; the puppy will smell its own scent and be encouraged to transfer toileting outside. As it eliminates, say "Hurry up"; this will train your dog to relieve itself on that command.

INTRODUCING OUTDOORS

WHATEVER THE SEASON, early experience outside the home is essential for your puppy. Make sure that your Poodle has had all the vaccinations it needs for meeting others, and equip it with identification. Meet with friends who have well-trained dogs to accustom your puppy to other dogs in a controlled way.

IDENTIFICATION

STANDARD NAME TAG
Engraved or canister tags carry vital information about your dog, including your address and telephone number and your vet's number. A tiny dab of nail varnish will prevent the canister from unscrewing.

Registration number is stored in this tiny microchip

PERMANENT METHOD
Inserted under the skin on the neck, a tiny transponder encased in glass can carry vital information about your dog. Data is read by a hand-held scanner. Painless, permanent tattoos, usually on the inside of the ear flap, are another option that may be available to you.

INTRODUCTION TO COLLAR AND LEAD

1 Collar and lead training can begin as soon as you take your puppy home. Start by letting it see and smell the collar. Then, avoiding eye contact, kneel beside your dog and, while distracting it with words, put on the collar. Reward with food, physical contact, and praise. Play enthusiastically with your puppy for a while, then take off the collar. Your Poodle puppy will soon learn that the collar is associated with rewards and will happily wear it.

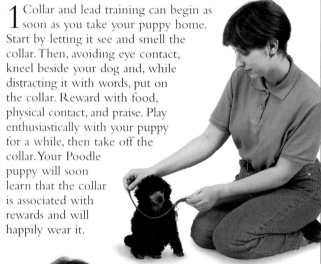

2 Once your puppy is content with wearing its collar, kneel in front of it and attach a lead. Keeping the lead slack, distract your puppy to one side with a toy or food reward. As it moves towards it, apply light tension to the lead. Reward your puppy with food or a toy and praise.

Puppy accepts collar and lead because it is distracted by toy

Encountering Other Dogs

Arrange for a friend who has a well-behaved, placid dog to meet you while you are out walking your puppy. Your friend should instruct his or her dog to sit while you and your puppy walk past. Reward your Poodle's calmness with food and praise. If you do not know people with dogs, you will find that other dog walkers are often quite prepared to help with this form of training. By creating situations where your dog meets others in an environment which you control, your Poodle learns that there is no need to be fearful of other dogs. Regular interaction with other puppies of a similar age will also help your dog to develop desirable canine social skills.

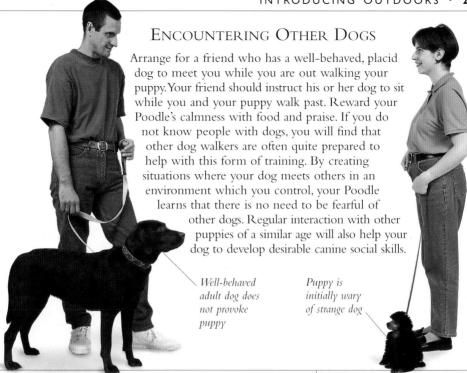

Well-behaved adult dog does not provoke puppy

Puppy is initially wary of strange dog

Meeting New People

Ask a friend to meet you and your puppy outdoors. Your friend should kneel when greeting your dog, to reduce the likelihood of it jumping up. Tell them to avoid eye contact with the puppy, as this can provoke an exaggerated, submissive response, most common in some Toy Poodle puppies. Remember to give your friend a food treat to reward your Poodle for its good behaviour.

Puppy will feel less threatened if it is greeted kneeling down

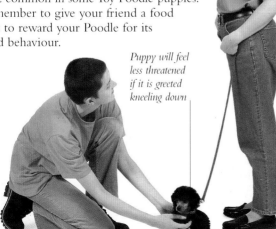

Essential Puppy Inoculations

At eight and 12 weeks, your puppy will be vaccinated by your vet for diseases such as parvovirus, distemper, leptospirosis, and hepatitis. Vets often advise that a puppy avoids contact with unfamiliar dogs for a couple of weeks to avoid possible infection. Contact with healthy dogs should continue, however, as this is vital for your dog's social development.

FIRST ROUTINES

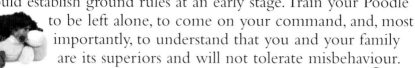

A PUPPY'S EARLY EXPERIENCES influence its adult personality, so you should establish ground rules at an early stage. Train your Poodle to be left alone, to come on your command, and, most importantly, to understand that you and your family are its superiors and will not tolerate misbehaviour.

ACCEPTING BEING LEFT ALONE

No matter how much you enjoy being with your new puppy, there will be times when you must leave it on its own. Train your young Poodle to accept that this is part of its routine by confining it to its crate with an interesting reward, such as a hollow toy filled with a little peanut butter or cheese spread. Then quietly walk away, giving the signal "Wait". Gradually accustom your dog to being left alone for longer periods of time.

Puppy will soon learn that hand signal means "Wait"

Puppy is content in crate because it has been rewarded with favourite toy

ASSERT YOUR LEADERSHIP

Some Poodles have a tendency to be pushy with their owners, to resist being groomed or handled, and even to snap at members of the household. Start grooming routines with your puppy from an early age and teach it the meaning of a stern "No!".

Owner uses body language and tone of voice to reprimand puppy

SEVERAL PUPPIES?

If you are rearing more than one puppy, train them individually for the most effective results. It is very difficult, even for highly experienced dog handlers, to maintain concentration on several lively puppies all at the same time!

COMING TO YOU ON COMMAND

1 Your dog's safety depends on you, and central to all training is its responsiveness in coming to you on command. Use positive training methods by rewarding your puppy when it responds to a command. Having taught your puppy to accept a collar and lead, put these on the puppy and kneel a short distance away, with the lead tucked securely under one knee. Hold an exciting toy in one hand; this will act as the reward for the puppy obeying your command.

Toy makes interesting reward for puppy

Initially puppy is distracted and ignores owner

2 Call your puppy's name in a clear, friendly tone to attract its attention. As it turns its head towards you, give the command "Come" and wave the toy to attract it. Do not apply tension to the lead; it is on to make sure that your puppy does not stray, not to reel it in. Encourage your puppy to come towards you for the reward.

Call your puppy by name in friendly tone of voice

When called, puppy turns around and sees toy

Praise your puppy after it responds correctly

3 Greet your puppy with open arms. Out of curiosity, it should walk towards you. As it moves, say "Good dog" in an enthusiastic voice. When the puppy reaches you, reward it with the toy. Never call your dog to discipline it – train it to understand that the command "Come" is always a positive one.

Puppy responds and walks towards toy

COME, SIT, DOWN, STAY

TRAINING YOUR PUPPY to come, sit, lie down, and stay down is most important for the safety of your dog and for harmonious relations with your family, friends, and outside the home. Poodles are exceptionally responsive to obedience training. Begin the basics as early as possible to make further training easier.

COME AND SIT

Maintain eye contact with puppy

1 Try to work in a quiet, narrow space such as a hallway, without any distractions. Holding the puppy on a loose lead, cheerfully call its name and let it see that you have a food treat in your hand. As it begins to move, give the command "Come". Be enthusiastic, and while your puppy walks towards you, praise it by saying "Good dog".

Lead is slack, but may be gently pulled to reinforce command

2 When your puppy reaches you, move the treat above its head. To keep its eye on the food, the puppy will naturally sit. As it does so, issue the command "Sit" and immediately give the reward. Repeat this exercise at least four times daily, before each meal, until your puppy responds to words alone.

Offer reward calmly to avoid over-excitement

Puppy sits willingly while watching treat

THE VALUE OF "NO!"

"No!" is one of the first, and most important, words your Poodle should learn. When your puppy understands its meaning, you can maintain control and prevent accidents. Just as you use a friendly voice and warm body language to reward your puppy and make training fun, adopt a stern tone and a dominant stance when issuing this reprimand. There is no need to shout; Poodles are superb at grasping inflection. Teach the phrase "No!" during general training, but no matter how frustrated you are, never use it to finish a session. Always end on a positive note.

Puppy stretches along floor to receive food treat

FOLLOW DOWN

1 With the puppy seated, kneel beside it, holding its collar with one hand, and place a food treat by its nose. If your puppy will not sit or tries to get up, firmly tuck its hindquarters under with your free hand and command "Sit".

2 Move the treat forwards and down in an arc, drawing your puppy as it follows the food with its nose. As it starts to lie down, give the command "Down". If the puppy refuses, gently raise its front legs into a begging position, then lower it down. Always reward your dog's compliance with praise.

Lead is secured under knee to maintain control

If puppy lunges at food rewards, use toy instead

3 Still holding the collar, continue to move the treat forwards and down until your puppy is lying completely flat. Then reward the puppy with the treat and praise. Do not praise excessively, however, since this can unduly excite your young Poodle and be counter-productive.

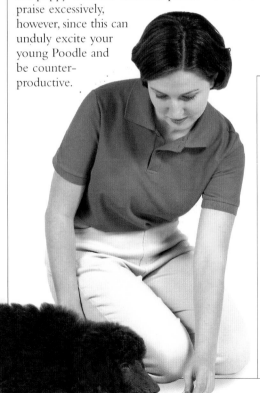

STAY DOWN

Having positioned your puppy down, give the command "Stay". With the lead still attached, and maintaining eye contact, walk in front, repeating "Stay". Instead of food rewards, which will attract your puppy to you, use a raised palm gesture; this will become a learned visual signal. Response to the "Stay" command is important in potentially hazardous situations.

Gradually extend length of "Stay" to a few minutes

WALKING TO HEEL

ENSURE THAT WALKING your dog is a pleasure by teaching it from an early age to walk willingly to heel. Some puppies initially train best for heelwork off the lead; others respond well to a lead from the start. Although Poodles are fine pupils, begin training in a quiet indoor space before graduating outside.

WALKING TO HEEL WITHOUT A LEAD

1 Kneel to the right of your alert, seated puppy. Holding its collar with your left hand, speak its name to attract its attention and show it a food treat or toy in your other hand.

2 Using the scent of the food to attract the puppy, get up and walk in a straight line while giving the command "Heel". Be ready to grasp the collar with your left hand and return your puppy to the correct position if it wanders. When you stop, command "Wait", then repeat the sequence.

Puppy eagerly follows reward

3 Keeping the treat low to prevent your puppy from jumping up, bend your knees and turn right, drawing the food reward around as you move. Repeat the command "Heel". Your puppy will naturally speed up to walk around you.

Train puppy to stay close to your leg

4 Left turns are more difficult. Hold the collar with your left hand and give the command "Steady". Place the reward in front of your puppy's mouth, then gently move it around to the left. The puppy should follow.

Puppy will turn to left to follow reward

Heelwork with a Lead

1 With the puppy to your left on a long training lead, tell it to sit. Hold the lead and a food treat in your right hand, and pick up the slack of the lead with your left.

Puppy watches owner intently

Seek eye contact as puppy waits for next command

2 Move forwards on your left foot and command "Heel". If your puppy strays too far ahead, give the lead a light jerk to pull it back.

3 With the puppy beside you in the heel position, offer it the reward and say "Good dog". Repeat the "Sit. Heel. Wait." sequence.

5 Once the right turn has been learned, begin left-turn training. Hold the treat in front of the puppy's nose to slow it down, while speeding up your circling movement to the left. Keep the puppy close to your left leg and give the command "Steady" as it follows you around.

4 After the puppy has learned how to walk to heel in a straight line, teach it to turn to the right by guiding it with the treat. Do not pull or get angry; build up confidence with praise.

Puppy slows down while concentrating on food reward

INDOOR TRAINING

ALTHOUGH YOUR POODLE loves being outdoors, it is likely to spend much of its time inside your home. Make sure that it understands basic house rules, and provide it with some space of its own. Give your Poodle plenty of time and attention, but always on your initiative, not on demand.

LEARNING TO WAIT PATIENTLY

Dogs were originally pack animals and followed a dominant pack leader. You should be this leader for your Poodle – you are the boss, who decides what happens and when. Some Toy and Miniature Poodles have a tendency to demand constant attention if they think they will receive it. Do not give in to these demands – it is you who should set the agenda. Make sure that you provide your Poodle with its own personal space, which should include its bed or crate. It will learn to rest here when you are busy.

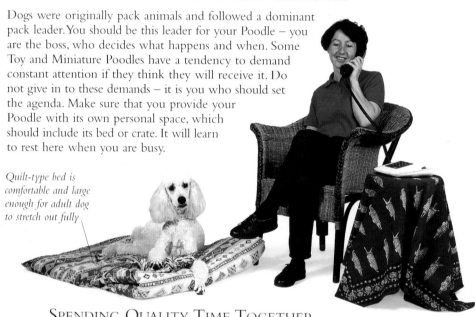

Quilt-type bed is comfortable and large enough for adult dog to stretch out fully

SPENDING QUALITY TIME TOGETHER

Nurturing the bond between you and your dog is not only enjoyable for both of you, but helps to reinforce basic obedience training. It is also essential to your dog's well-being and development. Set aside time each day to play games with your Poodle: these should provide a mixture of physical activity and mental stimulus. Be sure to vary the time of day and the type of play so that your dog will not expect a certain game at a particular time.

Playing together is fun, and keeps dog happy and alert

MEETING VISITORS IN THE HOME

Some Poodles, especially Toys and Miniatures, can be territorial; ensure that your dog is not a nuisance by training it to sit when a guest arrives. This will reduce the likelihood of territory guarding – most common in male dogs – and help control the inclination that some Poodles have to go wild with over-excitement. Ask visitors to ignore your pet as they arrive; this will encourage it to remain calm. Reward your dog's good behaviour with praise, a gentle stroke, or a food treat.

Dog is rewarded for sitting obediently

RELINQUISHING A FORBIDDEN ITEM

Poodles, like many breeds of dog, have a desire to hoard household items such as tea towels, socks, and slippers, often keeping them in their bed. Reduce the potential for such possessive behaviour by training your dog, using favourite food treats as rewards, to drop and surrender any item willingly on command.

UNDERSTANDING WHAT IS WRONG

Use body language as well as words to show your displeasure

Dogs will not know that they have done something wrong until this is made clear to them. Lying on a comfortable chair, for instance, seems perfectly natural to your Poodle, but may not be acceptable to you. Use an assertive stance and a stern voice to reprimand your dog when it does something that is not permitted. Act promptly; if you discipline your dog some time afterwards, it will understand only that you are angry, but not why.

BACK TO BASICS

Remember the principles of basic training and always return to them if your dog develops obedience problems later in life. Virtually all undesirable behaviour can be corrected if your dog responds to four simple commands – to come, sit, lie down, and stay. Poodles are more trainable than many other breeds and have a good but limited ability to understand language. Do not overload your dog with information; use short, sharp words, and issue commands only when you are certain that you can enforce them.

OUTSIDE THE HOME

FOR ITS OWN PROTECTION and the security of others, keep your Poodle under safe control in your own garden and further afield. When planning a holiday, make sure that your dog will be comfortable if left with other people. Always provide a healthy, hazard-free environment for your pet.

HOME AND AWAY

If you need to kennel your dog while you are away, visit recommended kennels and check them for cleanliness and security. Alternatively, consider a dog-sitting service; your vet may be able to supply you with details of a reliable agency.

Pack food, toys, bedding, and brushes for travel

BE CONSIDERATE TO OTHERS

Always obey local dog-control regulations, and clean up when your dog messes. Carry a supply of plastic bags or a "poop scoop" and use special waste bins if available. Do not let your dog be a nuisance to others.

CONTROL OUTDOORS

HEAD HALTER
A fitted head halter provides more control than a standard collar, and is especially useful for very strong-willed Poodles. If your dog pulls on its lead, its own momentum will pull its head downwards in an inhibiting manner.

HALF-CHECK COLLAR
This is the most common control for Poodles. Fit the collar so that the soft webbing lies around your dog's throat, with the chain at the back of the neck. A tug on the lead will tighten the collar painlessly.

MUZZLE
Apply a muzzle to obey local laws or to prevent your dog from biting. Use a basket variety in the correct size and properly adjusted to permit panting and barking. Never leave your muzzled dog unattended for lengthy periods.

SAFE TRAVELLING BY CAR

Train your dog from an early age to travel contentedly by car. Ensure its safety, and your own, by securing it in the back seat with a special canine seat belt that, like a child's harness, attaches to the standard seat-belt anchors. Alternatively, restrict your dog to the rear of an estate car fitted with a dog grille, or secure it in a transport container.

CAR DANGERS

Heatstroke is among the most common causes of preventable death in dogs. Since a dog cannot sweat other than through its pads, excess body heat can be reduced only by panting. In hot conditions, the body temperature rises swiftly, sometimes within minutes, and if there is no escape a dog can die. Never leave your dog in your car in warm or sunny weather – even when parked in the shade or with the window slightly opened. In cold weather, do not leave your dog in brilliant sunshine with the car engine running and the heater on high; this can be just as lethal.

PLANNING A SAFE AND SECURE GARDEN

The greatest hazard presented by your garden is the risk of escape. Check that all fencing is sturdy, gate latches secure, and that hedges have no gaps. Install wire mesh where necessary. Keep all garden chemicals safely locked away, and if you have outdoor lighting, ensure that no cables are exposed and may be chewed. To prevent damage to your lawn, train your dog to use a specific site as its toilet. Be certain to store all waste and any gardening tools securely out of reach, and do not establish plants that may be poisonous to dogs. Always watch your Poodle near a lit barbecue to ensure that it does not lick hot implements, and cover garden ponds to prevent your dog from paddling.

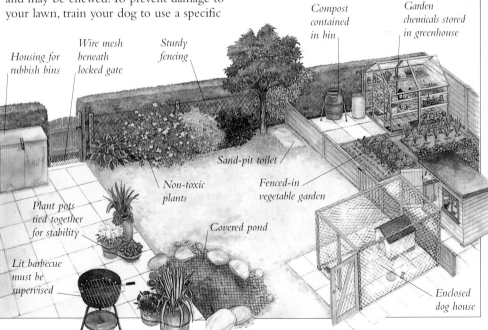

Housing for rubbish bins

Wire mesh beneath locked gate

Sturdy fencing

Compost contained in bin

Garden chemicals stored in greenhouse

Sand-pit toilet

Non-toxic plants

Fenced-in vegetable garden

Plant pots tied together for stability

Covered pond

Lit barbecue must be supervised

Enclosed dog house

CONSTRUCTIVE PLAY

REGARDLESS OF SIZE, Poodles have seemingly boundless physical and mental energy. Create activities that utilize these impressive abilities; games such as scent-trailing, retrieving, and carrying will stimulate and challenge your dog. Constructive play is fun, and helps to strengthen the bond between you and your pet.

GAME OF "HIGH FIVE"

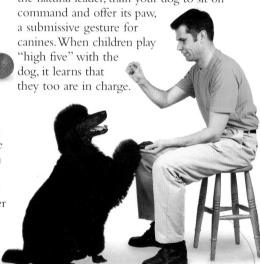

Some Poodles, especially small-sized males, can be surprisingly dominant with their human families. To reinforce that you are the natural leader, train your dog to sit on command and offer its paw, a submissive gesture for canines. When children play "high five" with the dog, it learns that they too are in charge.

Dog enjoys searching for familiar ball using sense of smell

SCENT-TRAILING

Exercise your Poodle's keen nose by showing it a toy, such as a rubber ball, with a distinctive odour. While out of sight, hide the item, then tell your dog "Find the ball". Encourage it to scent out the prize by using an excited tone of voice as it gets closer to the ball and a duller voice when it looks in the wrong direction. Outdoors, drag aniseed in a cloth bag to lay a scent trail, with a toy reward at the end.

PLAYING HIDE-AND-SEEK

Dexterous, quick-witted Poodle finds owner in hiding place

Poodles are very alert and thrive on mental stimulation. Keep your dog's faculties sharp by teaching it to play hide-and-seek. Begin by hiding while your dog watches, so it can easily find you on command. Progressively, make its search more complicated. Always reward your dog's success with lavish praise.

"Speak" and "Hush"

Small Poodles may be inclined to bark excessively. Pre-empt barking problems by training your dog, using food or toy rewards, to "Speak" on command. Once your dog has learned this, teach it to be quiet when you put your fingers to your lips and say "Hush". This useful routine helps to enforce household peace, and allows watchdog barking to be turned on and off at your discretion.

Poodles have natural instinct to retrieve

Dog will stop barking in response to "Hush" command and gesture

Retrieve on Command

Standard Poodles respond to "Fetch" training most readily; Miniatures and Toys require more time. Using praise as a reward, teach your dog to hold an object in its mouth, then to pick it up. Progress to the command "Fetch", sending your dog away to retrieve the item. Initially use a lead to ensure compliance. Once learned, the concept can then be applied to other objects.

Toys Belong to You

Poodles can be possessive with toys or food. Train your dog from an early age to release any item, initially for a food reward, then solely on the command "Drop". Play this game often to maintain your authority.

Dog willingly surrenders toy in exchange for treat

The Owner Always Wins

Forget about democracy when playing with your Poodle. You own all the toys, and you are always the winner. After games, have your dog see you collect all the toys and put them away. This reinforces that you are in charge, and also makes toys more valuable as rewards for good behaviour or when you leave your dog alone. Avoid games that are too stimulating, such as tug-of-war; your dog might want to win so much that it forgets some of its training. Ensure that play is still satisfying by finishing all games on a positive note, with food treats, stroking, or encouraging words.

GOOD CONTROL

LIKE ALL DOGS, your Poodle may at some time present you with behavioural problems. Some Poodles are particularly sensitive to unfamiliar situations; others may be provocative or socially dominant. Most difficulties can be overcome through proper care and training, and by establishing positive control.

HAPPILY OCCUPIED ALONE

No dog enjoys being left alone, including your energetic, gregarious Poodle. Always leave and return without a fuss, and exercise and feed your dog before you go out, to encourage rest. Give it a toy with a hollow centre that you have filled with a little cheese spread or peanut butter.

MEETING UNFAMILIAR PEOPLE

Miniature and Toy Poodles, in particular, can be surprisingly dominant. If your dog is aggressive towards strangers, ask a dog-loving friend to help act out social situations. Find a distance at which your dog remains calm, and reward its good behaviour. Gradually train it to accept other people at ever shorter distances, always reinforcing your control with commands.

Friend avoids eye contact with dog and squats down, to appear less threatening

Toy will be given as reward

Owner has trained his Cocker Spaniel to sit calmly on command

Standard Poodle curiously smells strange dog, but does not lunge

FRIENDLINESS WITH OTHER DOGS

A well-socialized dog will show curious interest rather than fear or hostility when meeting other dogs. If your Poodle is apprehensive or antagonistic, introduce it to a placid, even-tempered dog. Keep both dogs on a lead to maintain control. Find a distance at which your dog is at ease, and give it a reward. Over time, bring the two dogs closer together; always reward calmness, to teach your Poodle not to regard other dogs as a threat.

Dog is not alarmed when umbrella is opened

DEALING WITH A WILFUL DOG

As a rule, Poodles are wonderful family companions, but some, Toy and Miniature males in particular, can be wilful and disobedient. Be firm, and use psychological rather than physical discipline. If your dog does not respond to your commands, withdraw all rewards – and that includes your affection! Leave your dog on a lead indoors for controlled handling. If you are concerned about your Poodle's behaviour, contact your vet or local training club to arrange obedience lessons with a professional handler.

ACCEPTING NEW SITUATIONS

An alert breed, Poodles are usually intrigued by new sights and sounds; however, some dogs – especially Toys – may react nervously. If your dog is frightened by something unfamiliar, re-introduce it to the stimulus when far enough away not to be provoked. Reward calm behaviour with treats and reassuring praise. Over several weeks, gradually reduce the distance between your dog and the disturbing object, always rewarding composure.

DETERRENTS FOR CHEWING

Poodles often have a habit of chewing when bored; young dogs can be particularly destructive. When leaving your dog alone, give it a chewable toy. To teach it not to damage household articles, spray a potentially attractive object, such as a shoe, with a bitter-tasting but safe aerosol, available from pet shops.

Child looks away from dog while eating

Poodle knows it cannot have boy's treat

RESISTING TEMPTATION

Prevent begging by never giving your dog food while you are eating. Relenting with the occasional titbit will actually encourage this bad behaviour more than regular offerings. If your Poodle begs, command it to lie down, then look away. After you have finished eating, reward your dog's obedience with approving words or active play rather than food treats.

FOODS FOR YOUR DOG

ALTHOUGH MOST STANDARD Poodles love eating, Toys and Miniatures can be more fussy. Do not let your dog dictate its menu – it should be you who decides what it eats and when. Choose from the many commercially produced foods, or prepare well-balanced home-cooked meals.

CANNED FOODS

Moist, meaty canned foods come in a wide range of flavours and textures. Some are high in protein and are mixed with dry dog meal to provide added calories and vital carbohydrates; others are nutritionally complete on their own. Canned food will only stay fresh in the bowl for a short time.

Standard variety

Special formula for clinical conditions

"Stew" with gravy

Chunks in jelly

DRY MEAL

Crunchy dry meal is added to canned food to improve the texture, contribute fibre and fat, as well as exercise the jaws.

COMPLETE DRY FOODS

Complete dry foods are a convenient and practical way to feed Poodles, especially if you have two or more. By weight, standard brands contain about four times as many calories as canned food. In quantity, a Poodle needs less dry food than canned food and dog meal. Dry food produces less waste, making it easier to clean up after your dog.

HIGH-ENERGY
Puppies require nutrient-rich, easily digestible foods to sustain growth.

REGULAR
Adult formulas maintain mature dogs on a variety of activity levels.

LOW-CALORIE
Older, overweight, or sedentary dogs need less energy from their food.

TEETH-CLEANING
These large, crunchy chunks promote healthy gums and help control tartar.

SEMI-MOIST FOODS

These have three times the calories of canned foods and come in a variety of flavours, including cheese. A high carbohydrate content makes semi-moist foods unsuitable for diabetic dogs. Like dry foods, they can be left out all day so that your dog can eat at its own pace.

SUITABLE CHEWS

Poodles are avid chewers, and rawhide wrapped in the shape of a bone is an excellent chew, as is a hard, compressed biscuit chew. Avoid sterilized bones, which can fracture teeth.

Rawhide chew

TREATS AND BISCUITS

It is fun to give your Poodle snacks, but many are high in calories, and being too generous with them can result in an obese dog. Use these treats as rewards, and limit the amount given. The more snacks your Poodle receives, the smaller its regular meals should be.

BACON-FLAVOURED   SAVOURY RINGS   MEATY CHUNKS   LIVER ROUNDS

TABLE FOODS

As a general rule, a diet that is well balanced for us is also nourishing for canines. Never encourage begging by feeding scraps from the table, but prepare a special portion for your dog. White meat with pasta or rice is an excellent meal, but avoid strong spices.

Chicken is easily digested and lower in calories than red meat

When serving, mix rice or pasta with meat to ensure it is all eaten

MEDICAL DIETS

Some pet-food manufacturers produce a large variety of special diets to aid in the treatment of medical conditions ranging from heart disease to obesity. Your vet will recommend the best one for your dog.

Dry prescription food

Moist prescription food

HEALTHY EATING

PROVIDE YOUR POODLE with nutritious meals, in quantities appropriate for its age and energy requirements, and remember to supply plenty of fresh water to avoid dehydration. Although Poodles are not generally as food-orientated as many other breeds, prevent begging or obesity by feeding only at set times.

DIETARY NEEDS FOR ALL AGES

GROWING PUPPY

Puppies need plenty of nutrients for healthy growth. Feed four equal portions of semi-moist or canned puppy food daily. If preferred, offer two meals of breakfast cereal and milk, as well as two portions of canned or homemade food. Eliminate one cereal meal at three months and the other at six months.

A raised food bowl facilitates eating for this Standard Poodle

MATURE ADULT

The energy needs of an adult Poodle vary greatly and depend upon a number of factors, such as activity level, metabolism, and health. For example, a sedentary, neutered Poodle is prone to weight gain, and requires smaller portions than usual. Tie back the hair on the ears during meals.

FEEDING REQUIREMENTS

The figures given here represent an approximate guide only. Remember that each dog has its own specific nutritional needs, and that different brands of food vary in calories. Always provide a well-balanced diet to meet your dog's daily energy requirements. If you are uncertain of what is best for your Poodle, seek detailed professional advice.

DAILY ENERGY DEMANDS FOR TOY POODLES					
AGE	WEIGHT	CALORIES	DRY FOOD	SEMI-MOIST	CANNED/MEAL
2 MONTHS	1–2 kg (2–4.5 lb)	220	66 g (2 oz)	73 g (2½ oz)	110 g/37 g (4 oz/1 oz)
3 MONTHS	2–3 kg (4–6.5 lb)	320	96 g (3 oz)	107 g (3½ oz)	160 g/54 g (5½ oz/2 oz)
6 MONTHS	2½–5 kg (5–11 lb)	405	120 g (4 oz)	133 g (4½ oz)	200 g/68 g (7 oz/2½ oz)
TYPICAL ADULT	2½–5 kg (5–11 lb)	220–365	66–122 g (2–4 oz)	73–183 g (2½–6 oz)	110–183 g/37–62 g (4–6½ oz/1–2 oz)
ELDERLY (10 YEARS+)	2½–5 kg (5–11 lb)	180–300	54–90 g (2–3 oz)	60–100 g (2–3½ oz)	90–150 g/31–51 g (3–5 oz/1–2 oz)

ELDERLY POODLE

Generally, older dogs have lower energy needs and should be fed either smaller portions or low-calorie meals. Protein intake may also be reduced to help prevent obesity, which places undue strain on hind legs and organs such as the kidneys. Always provide plenty of fresh water to prevent dehydration, particularly if your Poodle is eating dry food.

FEEDING ROUTINES

It is vital to establish a strict routine for mealtimes. Train your dog to sit and stay when food is being served, and to eat only when allowed to do so. To reduce the risk of meal guarding, offer your puppy food from your hand, and stroke it while it is eating. Poodles can be fastidious eaters. Offer food for an hour and, if left untouched, take it away. Repeat until eating resumes.

Family enjoys meal without any canine interruptions

DAILY ENERGY DEMANDS FOR MINIATURE POODLES					
AGE	WEIGHT	CALORIES	DRY FOOD	SEMI-MOIST	CANNED/MEAL
2 MONTHS	2–3½ kg (4–7 lb)	395	118 g (4 oz)	132 g (5 oz)	198 g/67 g (7 oz/2 oz)
3 MONTHS	3–5 kg (6-10 lb)	495	148 g (5 oz)	165 g (6 oz)	248 g/84 g (8½ oz/3 oz)
6 MONTHS	4–12 kg (8–26 lb)	640	191 g (7 oz)	213 g (7½ oz)	320 g/109 g (11 oz/4 oz)
TYPICAL ADULT	5–14 kg (10–28 lb)	365–795	109–238 g (4–8 oz)	122–265 g (4–9 oz)	183–398 g/62–135 g (6½–14 oz/2–4½ oz)
ELDERLY (10 YEARS+)	5–14 kg (10–31 lb)	300–650	90–194 g (3–7 oz)	100–216 g (3½– 8 oz)	150–325 g/51–111 g (5–11 oz/2–4 oz)

DAILY ENERGY DEMANDS FOR STANDARD POODLES					
AGE	WEIGHT	CALORIES	DRY FOOD	SEMI-MOIST	CANNED/MEAL
2 MONTHS	3–5 kg (6–10 lb)	980	293 g (10 oz)	326 g (11½ oz)	490 g/167 g (17 oz/6 oz)
3 MONTHS	6–10 kg (12–30 lb)	1470	440 g (15½ oz)	490 g (17 oz)	735 g/250 g (26 oz/9 oz)
6 MONTHS	15–26 kg (30–52 lb)	1875	561 g (20 oz)	624 g (22 oz)	938 g/319 g (33 oz/11 oz)
TYPICAL ADULT	18–34 kg (36–68 lb)	960–1550	287–463 g (10–16 oz)	320–516 g (11–18 oz)	480–775 g/163–264 g (17–27 oz/6–9 oz)
ELDERLY (10 YEARS+)	18–34 kg (36–75 lb)	785–1270	235–380 g (8–13½ oz)	261–423 g (9–15 oz)	393–635 g/133–216 g (14–23 oz/5–7½ oz)

BASIC BODY CARE

SINCE POODLES' COATS require constant attention, common health problems can often be detected early during routine grooming. Examine your dog's eyes, ears, and mouth daily, and brush its teeth every week. Regularly trim the nails, and check the body thoroughly for any signs of irritation.

ENSURING CLEAR, HEALTHY EYES

Dampen cotton wool to avoid loose fibres

Healthy eyes are bright and clear, with dull pink mucous membranes. Bathe the area around the eyes daily using a fresh piece of cotton wool moistened with tepid salt water. If the eyes appear reddened or cloudy, arrange for a thorough veterinary examination. Yellow or green discharge is often a sign of infection and requires medical treatment. Also seek professional advice if your dog has watery eyes, or is inclined to blink or squint excessively.

CONTROL TARTAR

Poodles readily accumulate tartar on their teeth, which can lead to root infection and gum disease. Regular brushing, as well as specially-designed dry foods, compressed biscuit treats, and rawhide or nylon chews, all help to control tartar build-up. This dog's teeth and gums need veterinary care.

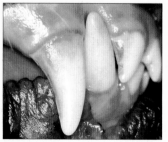

BRUSHING THE TEETH

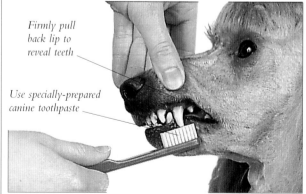

Firmly pull back lip to reveal teeth

Use specially-prepared canine toothpaste

Check daily for any debris lodged in the cheeks, the roof of the mouth, or between the teeth. Once a week, clean the teeth with a soft brush, working up and down to massage the gums. Do not use human toothpaste, which froths and is likely to be swallowed by your dog.

CLIPPER RASH

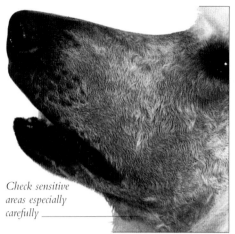

*Check sensitive
areas especially
carefully*

Some Poodles, especially dogs with lighter-coloured coats, are prone to clipper rash, a skin irritation that occurs after the coat is cut. After clipping, examine your dog thoroughly for signs of irritation or redness.

INSPECTING THE EARS

Check the ears daily for foreign material such as grass seeds, and for inflammation, wax, discharge, or odour. Remove excess wax carefully with a tissue, never probing too deeply. Hair growing in the ear canal should be extracted by hand at least once a week to prevent matting and infection.

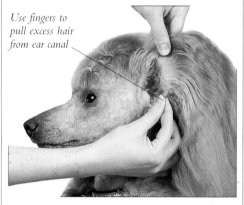

*Use fingers to
pull excess hair
from ear canal*

CUTTING THE NAILS

Command your dog to sit, and use a non-crushing "guillotine" clipper to cut the tip of the nail, avoiding the sensitive quick. On light-coloured Poodles with pale nails, the quick is visible; for dark nails, ask your vet where to cut. Reward your dog for calm conduct.

*Clip after bathing,
when nails are
soft and pliable*

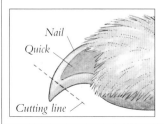

Nail

Quick

Cutting line

WHERE TO CLIP NAILS
The pink nail bed, or quick, contains blood vessels and nerves. To make clipping painless, always cut in front of the quick. If unsure, seek professional guidance on the correct technique.

ANAL HYGIENE

Excessive licking of the anal region or dragging of the hindquarters can mean that the scent-producing anal sacs are blocked, causing irritation and itching. Wearing protective gloves, squeeze the sacs empty, applying firm pressure from both sides. Use absorbent material to collect the fluid.

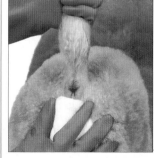

MAINTAINING THE COAT

THE COAT OF A POODLE does not moult, distinguishing it from the coats of most other dog breeds. Whatever style of clip you have chosen for your dog, the coat must be groomed daily to keep it looking clean and attractive. Bathe your dog regularly to maintain the condition of both its coat and skin.

ROUTINE GROOMING FOR POODLES

Thorough grooming at least once a week is essential for Poodles, as objects can easily become lodged in their curly, coarse coat. If left unbrushed for a prolonged period of time, a Poodle's coat will become tangled. Groom your dog in sequence from an early age. Larger dogs can lie on a special grooming table for ease of grooming.

GROOMING THE BODY
Part the hair along the spine using a straight-pinned bristle brush, then gently brush away from the parting and comb. Make a new parting a short distance away and repeat until the legs and sides are groomed.

Poodle submits willingly to grooming

Be gentle with thin leather of Poodle's ears

GROOMING THE EARS
Next, groom your Poodle's ears. Use a bristle brush for this. Poodles have hair that grows down the length of the ear canal, so gently pull out any visible hair with your fingers. Check your dog's ears for any foreign objects.

Brush upwards from the root of the hair

GROOMING AS A RITUAL

Some dogs, Miniatures and Toy Poodles especially, resent grooming. Try and avoid this problem by introducing a routine as soon as you acquire your dog. If your dog is strong-willed, command it to lie down, then lift its leg as a gesture of submission, then start grooming.

GROOMING THE HEAD AND TAIL
Next, holding your Poodle gently but firmly under the jaw, brush its topknot. This can be done with a metal comb with fairly widely spaced teeth. Finish grooming by brushing the hair on your Poodle's tail.

BATHING AND DRYING YOUR POODLE

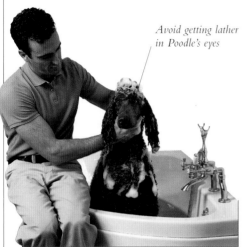

Avoid getting lather in Poodle's eyes

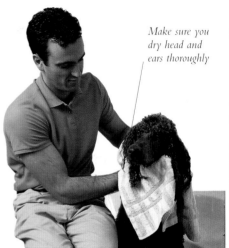

Make sure you dry head and ears thoroughly

1 Bathe a Toy or smaller Miniature Poodle in a large bowl or in the sink; Standards should be washed in the bath. Brush your Poodle before bathing to prevent matted hair from becoming hard when wet. Using a shampoo recommended by your vet, lather all of your dog except around the eyes. Make sure no water runs down into its ears. Clean your dog's face with a cloth. Rinse it thoroughly, paying special attention to the area under the legs.

2 Squeeze off any excess water while your dog is still in situ. Next, drape a bath towel over it and allow it to shake. Gently towel dry your Poodle's coat, making sure that the room is pleasantly warm and free from draughts. If allowed to dry naturally, your dog's coat will form tight, natural curls close to the skin. It is easier to brush knots out of dry hair. Remember to give your dog gentle words of praise while it is being bathed and groomed.

3 Dry off excess moisture with a hair dryer set at a moderate heat. Now is the best time to cut your Poodle's nails, as bathing makes them softer and less brittle. Finally, brush once more after drying to remove any loosened, dead hair. Finish off the grooming session by rewarding your dog with plenty of verbal praise and a food treat; this way, your Poodle will accept bathing more readily in the future.

Keep hair dryer at arm's length when blow drying

Be careful not to blow directly into Poodle's eyes

CLIPPING YOUR POODLE

POODLES' UNIQUE COATS can be clipped in a wide variety of styles. Cutting, trimming, and scissoring the hair into different shapes has become an art form – a kind of canine topiary. Choose a clipping style you like and learn the basics of coat trimming, or, if you prefer, have your dog's coat cut professionally.

BASIC EQUIPMENT

SCISSORS

COMB

CLIPPERS

BRUSH

Before you clip your Poodle's coat, buy some basic equipment and take advice from a professional groomer. Electric clippers may be bought from pet shops and should have a fine blade for the face and a coarser one for the body. A grooming table will make the job more convenient for you, and more comfortable and relaxed for your Poodle.

IMPORTANT CLIPPING TECHNIQUES

The following is a basic guide on how to clip your Poodle in a lamb trim. Seek advice before you embark on cutting your dog's coat, and have your first attempt professionally supervised. Do not cut your dog's coat too close – this can cause clipper rash, a painful skin irritation. Be extra careful when you clip the sensitive area around your dog's face.

1 Start from the corner of the ear and clip to the eye. Then clip from the voice box to the edge of the ear, along the muzzle and chin.

2 Separate toes by pressing from above and below. Use the side of the blade to trim the sides of the toe. Clip around the base of the foot.

3 Clip one third of the tail, against the lie of the hair, towards the base. Take care under the tail and around the sensitive anal area.

4 Clip behind the ears and topknot, down the neck and shoulders. Trim in the direction of hair growth over the chest and on underside.

CLIPPING STYLES

Because a Poodle's hair does not moult, it must be trimmed to keep it neat, clean, and easy to manage. Many clips started for purely practical reasons – shaving a dog's legs meant it could swim more efficiently in water, while the bracelets of hair left on the legs kept joints warm and insulated.

LION TRIM
Called the English saddle clip in the United States, the dog's face, throat, forelegs, and tail base are shaved, with puffs left on the forelegs. Hindquarters have a short blanket of hair with shaved bands around the legs.

LAMB TRIM
This is one of the easiest clips to learn. The coat is kept uniformly short, making it ideal for working dogs and bitches with puppies.

Puffs of hair surround joints on forelegs

Adult dogs can still be clipped in second puppy trim

SECOND PUPPY TRIM
This is often used for older puppies in the show ring. The front half of the dog is clipped like the lion trim, but the hindquarters are left without shaping, as in the lamb trim.

Pompoms on hindquarters are optional

CONTINENTAL TRIM
The classic Poodle clip; the face, throat, feet, and base of the tail are shaved. The hindquarters are also shaved, with pompoms of hair left on top. Puffs of hair (sometimes called bracelets) are left on the lower hind legs and forelegs.

BASIC HEALTH

YOUR POODLE DEPENDS on you for its good health. Since it cannot tell you that something is wrong, you must observe how your dog moves and behaves; any changes in activity or regular habits may be warning signs of problems. Arrange annual check-ups, and always consult your vet if you need advice.

EASY, GRACEFUL MOVEMENT

Poodles walk, trot, and run with natural grace and style, though excess weight will cause your dog to move less fluidly. It should be able to lie down and get up effortlessly – if it has difficulty getting up, limps, or bobs its head while walking, it may be in pain. Neck and back problems can affect some dogs at around six or seven years of age. Watch your Poodle during its daily activities for any anomalies in behaviour. If you think it is in discomfort, take it to a vet.

SOUND APPETITE AND EATING HABITS

Eating and toilet routines adopted during puppyhood are normally maintained throughout life and should remain constant. Even slight changes can be a sign of ill health, and should be referred to your vet. A reduced appetite can simply indicate boredom, but may also signal illness. Asking for food but not eating it can mean tooth pain; so too can sloppy eating – with food being dropped, then picked up and eaten. A heightened appetite without weight gain can indicate a thyroid problem. Increased thirst is always important and may be a sign of infection or conditions such as diabetes and liver or kidney disease. Seek veterinary advice if your dog starts to drink excessively or develops chronic diarrhoea or constipation.

Excessive eating may be medically significant

MOOD CHANGES

Dogs are creatures of habit, so watch out for any sudden changes in behaviour in your Poodle. It could be that there is a medical explanation for your dog's mood changes. Age slows down dogs, but if your Poodle is in pain, is suffering from poor circulation, or has a neurological problem, its temperament may be affected.

Behavioural changes during play may indicate medical problems

REGULAR HEALTH CHECKS

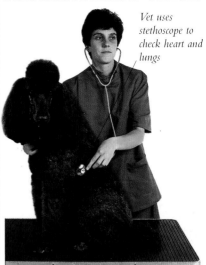

Vet uses stethoscope to check heart and lungs

Poodles tend to live longest when they are vaccinated against disease, checked annually by a vet, and treated for heart worms in countries where that is necessary. Many conditions, such as kidney and liver disease, may not be outwardly apparent, but can be diagnosed from blood samples. Problems are easiest to treat if detected early. Vets are the best source for information about your dog.

COPING WITH VISITS TO THE VET

Take your Poodle to the vet's surgery before it needs treatment, so that it can explore the premises. Ask your vet to give your dog a food treat while it is there, to make the next visit appealing. Repeat trips can be made less of a burden by taking out insurance cover on your Poodle's health. This guarantees that the most sophisticated treatments will be available for your dog without extra financial worry for you.

CARING FOR THE ELDERLY DOG

Your Poodle will not remain puppy-like forever. Dogs, like people, slow down with age. They may become hard of hearing and their vision may deteriorate. Devise activities that your dog will find less physically demanding – older dogs still enjoy playing, but are often less agile and energetic. Mental stimulation is the best antidote to ageing.

Older dog's coat has become flecked with grey hair

COMMON PROBLEMS

POODLES ARE ROBUST, healthy animals and have one of the highest life expectancies of any breed. However, like all dogs, they are susceptible to parasites, itchy skin, gastrointestinal complaints, and gum disease. Giving your dog a healthy diet and keeping it clean and well groomed reduces the likelihood of common ailments.

PARASITES

Poodles experience more problems with skin parasites in warmer climates. Fleas are the most common infestation. Check your dog's coat regularly for any sign of parasites.

FLEAS AND TICKS
Fleas live by biting dogs and feeding on their blood. They cause irritation and will make your Poodle scratch. Contact your vet for advice on flea-control preparations.

EAR MITE
These microscopic pests make homes in your dog's ears, which then become inflamed, sore, and itchy. This problem can be treated with insecticidal ear drops.

GUM DISEASE

All Poodles are susceptible to gingivitis, a disease where the gums become ulcerated and inflamed (see below). It leads to the gums receding, bacterial infection, and bad breath. Prevent it by brushing your dog's teeth on a regular basis from an early age.

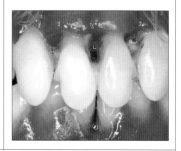

PERSISTENT LICKING AND SCRATCHING

Dogs may scratch themselves because of parasites, injuries, and allergies. Poodles with lighter-coloured coats are more prone to allergies than dogs with darker-coloured coats. Obsessive licking can lead to skin inflammation and hair loss. Licking of the anal region or dragging of the hindquarters across the floor may be due to your dog's anal sacs being blocked; this problem can be alleviated by periodically emptying them of fluid (see page 49).

Base of tail is licked excessively and may in turn become infected

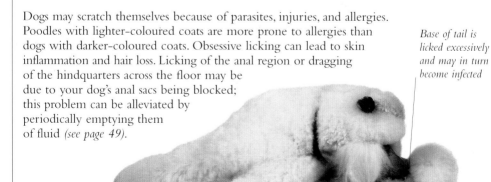

Typical Canine Complaints

With any breed, many health problems can be prevented – a better and more cost-effective option than treatment. Check your dog's skin routinely, especially the ears and between the toes. Groom and clip your Poodle's coat regularly. Clean teeth and gums once a week. Monitor your dog's weight to avoid potential obesity.

Ear Disorders
Humidity in the ear may lead to wax build-up, odour, and infection. Check your Poodle's ears routinely for unpleasant smells or inflammation and use wax removers recommended by your vet if necessary.

Painful Strains
Highly active Poodles, especially Standards, are particularly prone to muscle, ligament, tendon, and joint injury. Torn ligaments occur most commonly in the knee, while the hip joint can also be easily damaged.

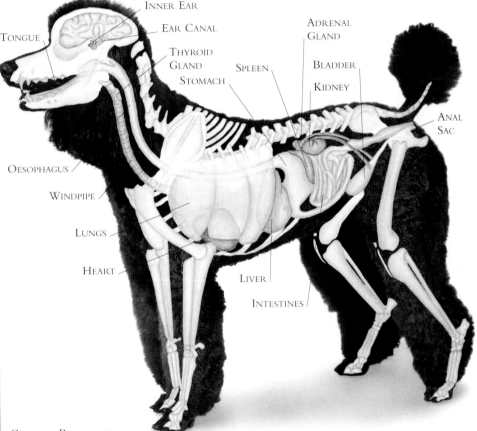

INNER EAR
EAR CANAL
TONGUE
THYROID GLAND
STOMACH
SPLEEN
ADRENAL GLAND
BLADDER
KIDNEY
ANAL SAC
OESOPHAGUS
WINDPIPE
LUNGS
HEART
LIVER
INTESTINES

Gastric Problems
It is by eating noxious or infected substances that Poodles most commonly pick up gastrointestinal problems. However, the most dangerous diseases of the stomach, such as parvovirus and distemper, can be prevented by routine vaccinations. If your dog has diarrhoea, vomits, or has difficulty passing a stool, contact your vet at once.

BREED-SPECIFIC PROBLEMS

THOUGH SELECTIVE BREEDING often brings about desirable traits, some hereditary ailments are also inevitably passed on. Poodles of all sizes are likely to suffer from problems concerning the stomach, skin, intestines, eyes, and joints. Toy Poodles may also have problems with the windpipe and hips.

EYE DISEASES

Like all dog breeds, Poodles can suffer from a variety of inherited eye diseases.

CATARACTS
Juvenile cataracts, formerly a problem in some Standards, are now less common thanks to selective breeding. The eye shown above is that of an older dog – the cloudy effect indicates a cataract.

GLAUCOMA AND ENTROPION
Glaucoma, an increase in pressure in the eye, sometimes affects Miniature Poodles. Standard dogs can be prone to entropion, where the lower eyelid rolls in on itself.

RETINAL DISEASE
Progressive retinal atrophy affects Toy and Miniature Poodles. It is a disease in which the retina has fewer and thinner blood vessels than normal, leading to partial or total blindness.

GASTRIC TORSION

A few Standard Poodles suffer from gastric torsion, in which the stomach twists round on itself (*shown right*) and gas builds up, putting pressure on the diaphragm. Symptoms include bloating and excessive thirst. Seek emergency help.

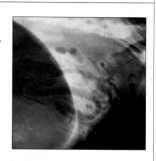

LEGG-PERTHE'S DISEASE

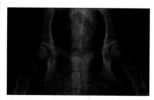 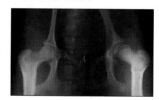

Some Toy Poodles inherit a painful condition known as Legg-Perthe's disease, where the head of the femur loses its blood supply and effectively "dies". The X-ray on the left shows two healthy, smooth hip joints. The X-ray on the right shows a diseased joint. The right hip joint is slightly misshapen; it has become hard, abrasive, and inflamed. The complaint can be corrected by surgery, during which the rough part of the femur is cut off.

IMPORTANCE OF HEALTH SCREENING

Responsible Poodle breeders have their stock thoroughly examined so that the presence of the most common hereditary diseases of the eye, hip, and skin can be detected. These breeders will be pleased to give you copies of all the appropriate health screening certificates if you buy a puppy from them. Scientists predict that in the near future it will be possible to use DNA "fingerprinting" on tiny blood samples in order to determine whether an individual dog is carrying genes that could cause it to suffer from a potentially devastating inherited disease.

OTHER DISORDERS MORE COMMON IN POODLES

All breeds of dog are prone to some genetic disorders. None of these conditions are very common and most are restricted to certain lines. Due to breed associations and vets working together, much is known about the Poodle's inherited medical problems.

SEBACEOUS ADENITIS
The lubricating oil glands in your Poodle's skin may become inflamed, a condition known as sebaceous adenitis. Your Poodle's hair will appear thin, and light coats may look darker. Check your dog regularly for any sign of skin problems.

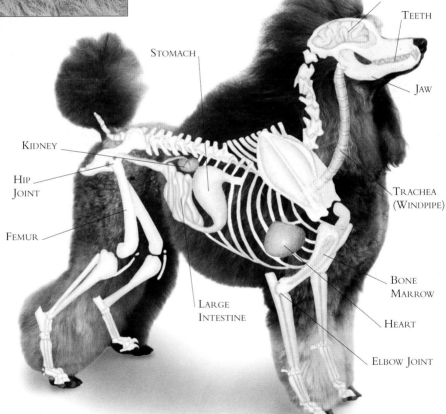

BRAIN
TEETH
STOMACH
JAW
KIDNEY
HIP JOINT
FEMUR
TRACHEA (WINDPIPE)
LARGE INTESTINE
BONE MARROW
HEART
ELBOW JOINT

IRRITABLE BOWEL SYNDROME
Also known as colitis, an inflammation of the large intestine, this condition is found in some Poodles. Dogs may suffer from diarrhoea that may contain mucus and blood. Vomiting may also be a symptom.

TRACHEAL COLLAPSE
Most common in small Toy Poodles, this occurs when the windpipe is softer than normal and collapses. Surgery to put in an artificial windpipe is sometimes necessary.

FORESEEING DANGERS

THE STANDARD POODLE'S sensible personality makes it less inclined than Miniatures or Toys to behave rashly. Nevertheless, always monitor your dog's activities, especially outdoors, and never leave it alone in a situation where it may put itself in danger. Remember that cars cause more dog deaths than anything else.

ENSURING SAFETY WITH YOUR POODLE

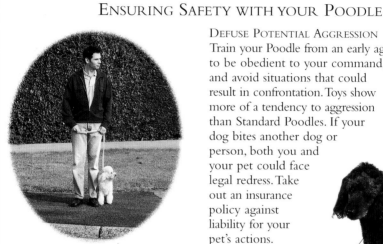

DEFUSE POTENTIAL AGGRESSION
Train your Poodle from an early age to be obedient to your command, and avoid situations that could result in confrontation. Toys show more of a tendency to aggression than Standard Poodles. If your dog bites another dog or person, both you and your pet could face legal redress. Take out an insurance policy against liability for your pet's actions.

INSTIL ROAD SENSE
Poodles are naturally enthusiastic, and even the best-trained dog may dart out onto a road if excited. Always walk your dog on a lead where there is potential danger.

Maintain control of your Poodle in social situations by keeping it on a lead

Unleashed dog causes a nuisance by chasing and barking at cyclist

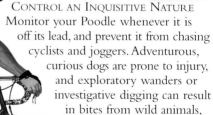

CONTROL AN INQUISITIVE NATURE
Monitor your Poodle whenever it is off its lead, and prevent it from chasing cyclists and joggers. Adventurous, curious dogs are prone to injury, and exploratory wanders or investigative digging can result in bites from wild animals, stings, and irritations caused by plants and insects. Keep your Poodle away from known dangers, including water, and carry a first-aid kit in case of emergencies.

COMMON POISONS AND CONTAMINANTS

IF INGESTED		ACTION
Slug and snail bait Strychnine rat poison Illegal drugs Aspirin and other painkillers Sedatives and antidepressants	Warfarin rat poison Lead (batteries, etc.) Antifreeze	Examine any packaging to determine its contents. If the poison was swallowed within the last two hours, induce vomiting by giving crystals of washing soda, a "ball" of wet salt, or 3 per cent hydrogen peroxide by mouth. Consult your vet immediately.
Caustic soda Dishwasher granules Paint remover or thinner Kerosene or petrol Drain, toilet, or oven cleaner	Chlorine bleach Laundry detergents Wood preservatives Polishes	Do not induce vomiting. Give raw egg white, bicarbonate of soda, charcoal powder, or olive oil by mouth. Apply a paste of bicarbonate of soda to any burns in the mouth. Seek urgent medical advice from your veterinarian.
IF IN CONTACT WITH THE COAT		ACTION
Paint Tar Petroleum products Motor oil		Do not apply paint remover or concentrated biological detergents. Wearing protective gloves, rub plenty of liquid paraffin or vegetable oil into the coat. Bathe with warm, soapy water or baby shampoo. Rub in flour to help absorb the poison.
Anything other than paint, tar, petroleum products, and motor oil		Wearing protective gloves, flush the affected area for at least five minutes, using plenty of clean, tepid water. Then bathe the contaminated coat thoroughly with warm, soapy water or mild, non-irritating baby shampoo.

EMERGENCY TREATMENT

With any case of poisoning, look for signs of shock, and give essential first aid as required. Contact your vet or local poison-control centre for specific advice, and begin home treatment as quickly as possible, preferably under professional guidance by telephone.

PROTECTING YOUR DOG

Poodles are naturally curious, and will investigate anything. Keep all household, garden, and swimming-pool chemicals securely shut away from your dog, and never give an empty container as a chew toy. Switch off electrical sockets when not in use, and, if you have puppies, spray visible electrical cords with a safe but bitter-tasting aerosol, available in pet shops. Ensure that your home provides a healthy environment for your puppy or adult dog.

Puppy should not be given container as toy

PREVENT SCAVENGING

Scavenging is a part of natural canine behaviour that should be discouraged. Train your Poodle to drop objects on command, and prevent it from eating bones and other animals' droppings. Also worm your Poodle regularly.

EMERGENCY FIRST AID

A HOME FIRST-AID KIT should contain all the items needed for initial treatment of minor injuries. More serious emergencies are less common, but with an understanding of some basic first-aid techniques, such as artificial respiration and cardiac massage, you could save your dog's life.

FIRST-AID PRINCIPLES AND BASIC EQUIPMENT

The fundamentals of human first aid also apply to dogs. Your objectives are to preserve life, prevent further injury, control damage, minimize pain and distress, promote healing, and get your dog safely to a vet for professional care. Have a fully stocked first-aid kit ready to hand and use it to treat minor wounds, once you are certain that there are no more serious, life-threatening problems to deal with.

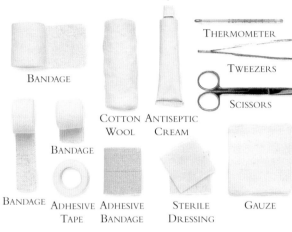

THERMOMETER

TWEEZERS

SCISSORS

BANDAGE

COTTON ANTISEPTIC
WOOL CREAM

BANDAGE

BANDAGE ADHESIVE ADHESIVE STERILE GAUZE
TAPE BANDAGE DRESSING

HOW TO ASSESS AN UNCONSCIOUS DOG

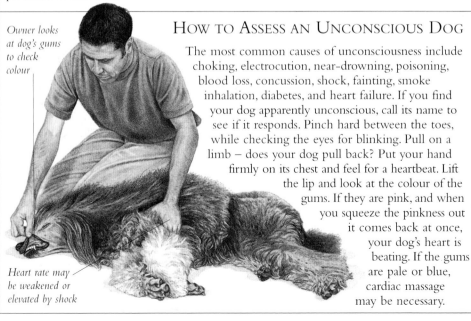

Owner looks at dog's gums to check colour

The most common causes of unconsciousness include choking, electrocution, near-drowning, poisoning, blood loss, concussion, shock, fainting, smoke inhalation, diabetes, and heart failure. If you find your dog apparently unconscious, call its name to see if it responds. Pinch hard between the toes, while checking the eyes for blinking. Pull on a limb – does your dog pull back? Put your hand firmly on its chest and feel for a heartbeat. Lift the lip and look at the colour of the gums. If they are pink, and when you squeeze the pinkness out it comes back at once, your dog's heart is beating. If the gums are pale or blue, cardiac massage may be necessary.

Heart rate may be weakened or elevated by shock

ARTIFICIAL RESPIRATION AND CARDIAC MASSAGE

Do not attempt to give artificial respiration or heart massage unless your dog is unconscious and will die without your help. If your dog has been pulled from water, suspend it by its hind legs for at least 30 seconds to drain the air passages. If it has been electrocuted, do not touch it until the electricity is turned off. If it has choked, press forcefully over the ribs to dislodge the object. Never put yourself at risk; if possible, share first-aid procedures with someone else or have them telephone the nearest veterinarian and arrange transport.

Tongue is pulled forwards and debris removed

Hold muzzle shut and seal your mouth over dog's nostrils

1 Place your dog on its right side, ideally with its head slightly lower than the rest of its body, to send more blood to the brain. Clear the airway by straightening the neck, pulling the tongue forwards, and sweeping the mouth with two fingers to remove any saliva or obstructions. Also clear the nose of excess mucus. If you cannot hear your dog's heart, begin cardiac massage immediately.

2 Close the mouth, hold the muzzle with both hands, and place your mouth around the nose. Blow in until you see the chest expand, then let the lungs deflate. Repeat this procedure 10–20 times per minute, checking the pulse every 10 seconds to make sure that the heart is beating.

Pumping forces blood towards brain

ALWAYS LOOK FOR SHOCK

Shock is a potentially life-endangering condition that occurs when the body's circulation fails. It can be caused by vomiting, diarrhoea, poisons, animal bites, a twisted stomach, bleeding, and many other illnesses or accidents, and onset may not be apparent for several hours. The signs include pale or blue gums, rapid breathing, a faint or quickened pulse, cold extremities, and general weakness. Treating shock takes precedence over other injuries, including fractures. Your priorities are to control any bleeding, maintain body heat, and support vital functions. Unless shock is the result of heatstroke, wrap your dog loosely in a warm blanket, elevate its hindquarters, stabilize breathing and the heart if necessary, and seek immediate medical advice. If your dog begins to panic, try to prevent it from injuring itself further, and take care not to get bitten.

3 If the heart stops, start cardiac massage. For Standard Poodles and larger Miniatures, place the heel of one hand just behind the left elbow, then the heel of the other on top. Press down and forwards, pumping 80–100 times per minute. For Toys, pinch the chest between the thumb and fingers, squeezing together and forwards. Alternate 20–25 cardiac massages with 10 seconds of mouth-to-nose respiration until the heart beats, then continue resuscitation until breathing begins.

MINOR INJURY AND ILLNESS

EVERY OWNER SHOULD KNOW how to administer medicines and other basic treatment to their dog in the event of accident or illness. Injuries to ears and paws, from fights or sharp objects, are not uncommon, and may require prompt bandaging and precautionary restraint before a vet is called.

APPLYING AN EMERGENCY BANDAGE TO THE EAR

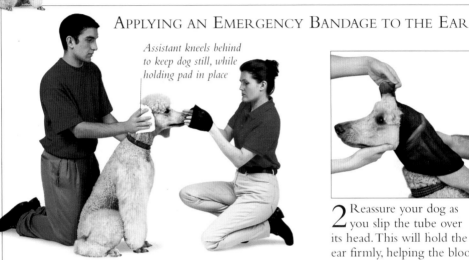

Assistant kneels behind to keep dog still, while holding pad in place

1 While an assistant soothes and steadies your dog, apply clean, preferably non-stick, absorbent material to the wound. Take care that you are not bitten through fright. Cut a tube from a pair of tights and slip it over your hands.

2 Reassure your dog as you slip the tube over its head. This will hold the ear firmly, helping the blood to clot, while also allowing air into the wound. Ensure that the windpipe receives no undue pressure.

BANDAGING A WOUNDED PAW

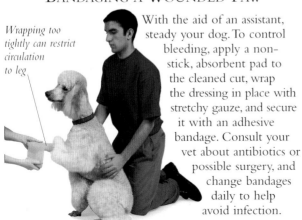

Wrapping too tightly can restrict circulation to leg

With the aid of an assistant, steady your dog. To control bleeding, apply a non-stick, absorbent pad to the cleaned cut, wrap the dressing in place with stretchy gauze, and secure it with an adhesive bandage. Consult your vet about antibiotics or possible surgery, and change bandages daily to help avoid infection.

3 If necessary, secure the tube at each end with tape to prevent your Poodle from pulling off the bandage. Although this will provide excellent temporary cover, have your vet examine the injury as soon as possible.

ADMINISTERING MEDICINES

Pill is disguised in favourite food

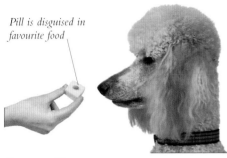

GIVING A PILL
Tablets can be hidden in food. Alternatively, open your dog's mouth, drop the pill as far back as possible, hold the muzzle closed, and stroke the neck to induce swallowing.

GIVING LIQUIDS
If mixing medicine into food is not practical, syringe it into the mouth, but not down the throat, where it may enter the windpipe. Hold the jaws shut until your dog swallows.

IMPROVISING A MUZZLE

1 Even the most loving animal is capable of reflex biting if in pain. Unless its breathing is impaired, restrain your dog by slipping a loop of any soft material, such as tights, gauze, or a tie, around its muzzle.

2 With the loop in place, tighten it gently. Then bring both lengths of material down and cross them under the jaws. If your dog is agitated or upset, speak to it in a relaxed, comforting tone as you proceed.

3 To complete the process, wrap the material round the back of the ears and tie the ends securely in a knot. With the emergency muzzle firmly fastened, you can then safely examine your dog and attend to its specific injuries.

REMOVING FOREIGN OBJECTS

Poodles love being outdoors, but their curly, coarse coats attract foreign objects such as grass seeds, thorns, and other plant material. If left, these items can cause discomfort and pain. Get into the habit of checking your Poodle's body regularly for foreign objects, especially between the toes and ears, and, in females, around the vulva. Use a pair of tweezers or your fingers to remove this material before it penetrates the skin. If you cannot remove the item without hurting your dog, consult your vet.

EARLY BREED ORIGINS

THERE ARE SEVERAL theories as to the Poodle's exact country of origin, with historical evidence pointing to Germany, France, and Russia. Originally bred as a large water dog for hunting and retrieving, the Poodle was also miniaturized, and became a popular pet dog with the noble families of Europe.

HISTORY OF THE POODLE

HISTORICAL REFERENCES

Paintings and literary references from the early 16th century document the existence of a breed closely resembling the modern Poodle. By the time of Thomas Gainsborough's 18th-century painting of his daughters with a Poodle (*right*), the breed was firmly established, not only as an excellent hunting dog, but also as a fashionable lap dog.

"FANCY" WATER DOG
This 18th-century painting by Jean-Baptiste Oudry (*left*) shows the Poodle in its working role. Although it was famous as a water dog in Continental Europe, the Poodle was rivalled by retrievers such as Spaniels in England, where it was known as a "fancy" dog through-out the 19th century.

OUDRY'S "ZAZA, THE DOG"

PORTRAIT BY GAINSBOROUGH

ANCESTORS AND RELATIVES

The Poodle's ancestors were the German gun dog, the Pudel, and the French retriever, the Barbet. Although John Chalon's picture of Poodle clippers in Paris shows that the modern Poodle was established by the early 19th century, it was not until 1876 that the Poodle was classified as a distinct breed. Relatives of the modern Poodle include the Spanish, Irish, and Portuguese Water Dogs and the Hungarian Puli. Near relations to Miniature and Toy Poodles include smaller breeds like the Bichon Frise and the Bolognese.

CHALON'S "THE DOG CLIPPERS", 1820

BICHON FRISE
*Popular in the
16th-century French
royal court, and as
a circus performer*

BOLOGNESE
*Originating from Italy, descriptions
of this companion breed were
first recorded in the 13th century.
Its coat is not as strongly curly
as the Poodle's*

PORTUGESE WATER DOG
*Known as a "specialist"
water dog, which is
used to retrieve lost
nets, fishing gear, and
fish. Clipped like a
Poodle at the rear*

SPANISH WATER DOG
*Multi-purpose breed
that assists in
herding, hunting,
and fishing. Bred
in Southern Spain,
primarily for
goat-herding*

HUNGARIAN PULI
*Responsive, obedient, and
virtually waterproof; used for
sheep-herding and retrieving
from water*

RECENT HISTORY

IN MODERN TIMES, the Poodle has become one of the most popular dog breeds. Until recently, it was a valued performer in circus acts, because of the ease with which it mastered new tricks. The Poodle's distinctive looks have made it a popular subject for paintings, curios, and *objets d'art*.

CHANGING FASHIONS

A 1919 POSTCARD OF POODLE COAT STYLES

CURLY AND CORDED POODLES

At the turn of the 20th century, it became very popular to allow a Poodle's coat to grow into long cords, often stretching to the ground. Pomades would be applied to the coat to produce cords with a tight twist. The fashion never took over entirely, and brushed out, clipped coats similar to those seen today were still popular. With the advent of mechanical clippers in the 1920s, this trend went into a steady decline.

CIRCUS POODLES

In the 18th and 19th centuries, the Poodle could be seen in circuses throughout Europe and America performing a variety of tricks; the breed's ability to learn anything from walking on its hind legs and skipping to performing card tricks and even playing dominoes made it extremely popular. The French artist Henri de Toulouse-Lautrec was to immortalize the Poodle in this role in a series of drawings and paintings.

"IN THE CIRCUS" BY TOULOUSE-LAUTREC

CHURCHILL WITH HIS POODLE, RUFUS I

A MOST POPULAR BREED

By the middle of the 20th century, the Poodle's charm and appearance had made it one of the world's best-loved dog breeds. In Britain, Winston Churchill's public affection for his pet Poodle, Rufus I, and its successor Rufus II, increased the dog's popular appeal, while in the United States, a Toy Poodle tucked under one arm became the ultimate high-status accessory for any aspiring Hollywood starlet.

POODLE COLLECTORS' ITEMS

The Poodle's position as one of the world's favourite dogs is reflected in the vast array of items that feature it. The breed's unique appearance and endearing nature have caused it to be represented in everything from priceless paintings and fine jewellery to mass-produced, utilitarian items with only novelty value and kitsch appeal.

POODLE MONEY-BOX
This early 20th-century whimsical English money-box, shaped like a Poodle begging, epitomizes the ceramic items that feature the breed.

POODLE ART
The Impressionist painter Pierre Bonnard (1867-1947) conveys the breed's playfulness and fun-loving nature in this picture, entitled "Two Poodles".

POODLE JEWELLERY
Poodles are often associated with luxury. Items such as this diamond-encrusted gold brooch, which dates from the turn of the century, are very collectable today.

POODLE CROSSBREEDS

Breeders have crossed the Poodle with a wide range of dogs in their search for new and interesting varieties. There have been some very successful combinations. The Pekepoo is a cross between the Poodle and the Pekingese; the Labradoodle is a mixture of Poodle and Labrador Retriever, sometimes used as a guide dog. The Pudelpointer is a hybrid of the Poodle and various kinds of Pointers, and the Cockerpoo is a combination of the Poodle and American Cocker Spaniel.

Poodle stock is most noticeable in texture of Cockerpoo's coat

PUDELPOINTER

COCKERPOO

REPRODUCTION

STANDARD POODLES HAVE few fertility problems and produce large litters, whereas Miniatures and Toys have correspondingly less offspring and may need more coaxing to mate. Consider breeding puppies from your Poodle only after consulting your vet, and enlist professional help during the delivery.

THE MATING INSTINCT

Healthy males as young as 10 months old are suitable for mating. However, it is best to wait until a female is about two years of age, usually in her third oestrous cycle, when she is emotionally prepared for the demands of a litter. Ovulation usually occurs 10–12 days after the first sign of bleeding and swelling of the vulva. It is often advisable to take the female to the male's home, where he is more likely to perform as expected.

PREGNANCY DIAGNOSIS

Ovulation – the prime time to conceive – is accurately assessed by an increased level of the hormone progesterone in the blood. However, pregnancy cannot be confirmed by blood or urine tests. Ultrasound at three weeks or a physical examination slightly later remain the best means of diagnosis.

Ultrasound scan shows several puppies in womb

DEALING WITH MISMATING

Mismatings can be avoided by keeping a watchful eye on your bitch when in season, by using tablets or injections to prevent ovulation, or by spaying. If an unwanted mating does occur, contact your vet at once. A pregnancy can be terminated, usually within three days of mating, with a hormone injection. This will induce an immediate repeat season, demanding renewed vigilance for 8–15 days after the beginning of vaginal discharge.

SPECIAL NEEDS OF AN EXPECTANT BITCH

During the first month of pregnancy, your bitch should continue to exercise freely. Thereafter, the increasing weight of the litter will naturally make her slower and less agile. At this stage, swimming is good exercise, but avoid cold water. After the sixth week, food intake should be gradually increased, so that by the expected delivery date the bitch will be eating 30 percent more than usual. The diet should include an adequate amount of calcium and phosphorus for bone growth.

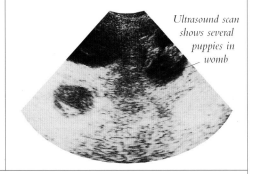

MALE AND FEMALE REPRODUCTIVE SYSTEMS

A bitch comes into season twice yearly, is fertile for three days during each cycle, and is only receptive to mating during these periods. Males, however, willingly mate all year round. For the female, ovulation continues throughout life and there is no menopause, although breeding in later years is risky. Pregnancy lasts for about 63 days.

RESPONSIBLE BREEDING

If planning to breed from your Poodle, seek advice from your vet or from a reputable breeder. Ensure that the prospective parents have the physical and emotional attributes that will enhance the breed. For example, both should be screened for common inherited diseases or conditions involving the eyes and joints. Remember, you will have to find each puppy a suitable home.

PREVENTING PREGNANCY

Neutering is the most effective, and safest means of preventing pregnancy. Females have the ovaries and the uterus removed, followed by a week's rest. The male's operation is easier; a small incision is made in the scrotum and the testicles are removed.

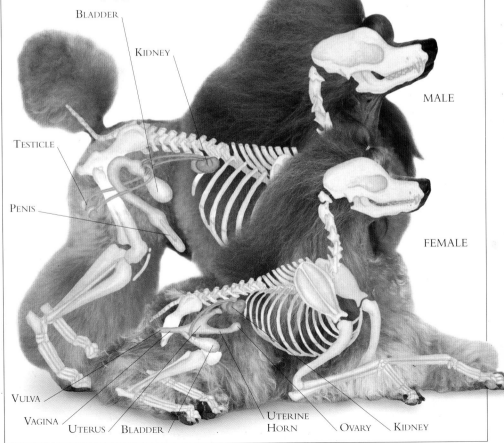

BLADDER

KIDNEY

MALE

TESTICLE

FEMALE

PENIS

VULVA

VAGINA   UTERUS   BLADDER

UTERINE HORN   OVARY   KIDNEY

PRE- AND POST-WHELPING

SEVERAL WEEKS BEFORE her puppies are due, introduce the expectant mother to her whelping box and arrange for your vet to be available in case of problems. Although Poodles seldom have birth difficulties, it is best to have experienced help both at the delivery and later, for after-care of weak puppies.

INTRODUCING A WHELPING BOX

Familiarize the mother-to-be with her whelping box a few weeks before the expected delivery. Standard Poodles need a box at least 1.2 m (4 ft) long and deep, and made of plywood to prevent damage from birth fluids. Three sides should be 45-50 cm (18-20 in) high to stop the puppies escaping, and the fourth side should have a lockable opening to allow the mother easy access. Miniatures and Toys need a box 80 cm (31 in) long with sides 25-30 cm (10-12 in) high. Collect plenty of newspaper to line the box and to serve as bedding.

DELIVERY CARE

If you have never been present at a birth, ask an experienced dog breeder to attend, and inform your vet when labour begins. Keep the room temperature at around 25° C (77° F). If after two hours your bitch does not produce a puppy, contact your vet once again for advice. The puppy's position may require manipulating to facilitate delivery. Poodles usually produce well-proportioned puppies that seldom need delivery by Caesarean section. Put a warm, towel-covered hot-water bottle in a cardboard box and place each newborn puppy inside. Also use this box if you need to transport mother and puppies to the veterinary clinic.

SIGNS OF IMMINENT BIRTH

Your bitch may refuse food just before she goes into labour. She will restlessly seek out her whelping box and start to tear up the bedding, preparing a nest for her puppies. Her body temperature will drop from the normal 38° C (101° F) to as low as 36° C (97° F), and she may pant. When her waters break and contractions begin, a membrane balloon appears in the vulva and a puppy is imminent. Avoid any distractions, and keep other animals and strangers away during the labour.

Expectant mother tears up bedding to prepare nest for her litter

CARE OF THE NEW LITTER

Towel-dry each puppy after it is delivered and clear its nose of mucus; all newborns should squeal and wriggle. During whelping, offer the mother warm milk. Let her rest after labour has ended and all placentas have been delivered. Place each puppy by a teat to suckle. The bitch will also need plenty of food in the coming weeks – at peak lactation, up to four times her normal intake.

Young puppies suckle eagerly as mother guards her brood

ASSISTING A WEAK OR ABANDONED PUPPY

BOTTLE-FEEDING
In large, healthy litters where there is not enough maternal milk to feed all the puppies, or when the mother is incapacitated, use canine milk formula as a supplement. Seek your vet's advice on correct quantities, and initially bottle-feed around every two to three hours.

HELPING TO SUCKLE
About one in seven puppies is born relatively small and weak. Runts are often the least healthy of the litter and, if left to nature, frequently die within a few days. To aid survival, place frail puppies near teats that offer the best supply of milk. If the puppy still does not suckle, it may have to be bottle-fed.

GROWING UP TOGETHER

After about three weeks, the maturing puppies will begin to explore their new environment; by 12 weeks, their senses are fully developed. Handle and groom all puppies often, so they learn to accept being touched by humans, but do not upset the protective mother. If puppies are gently exposed to other animals, people, sights, and sounds during this vital stage in their development, they are more likely to become well-adjusted, sociable adults.

All silver Poodles are born black; silver hairs begin to show through at around three weeks of age

PARTICIPATING IN A SHOW

TAKING PART IN a dog show can be very rewarding, but both you and your Poodle should be fully prepared. At most shows, Poodles are evaluated not only against the other dogs that are competing, but also against the judge's interpretation of the ideal physical and personality characteristics for the breed.

Owner gives Poodle final trimming before judge's inspection

MEETING SHOW STANDARDS

First, visit a show without your dog, to see exactly what goes on. Working trials require dogs trained to perform at a high level of obedience, whereas kennel-club events demand only beauty and character. Assess whether your dog matches the published breed standard applicable to your country. It should also be outgoing and enjoy being handled by strangers. Events vary from informal village shows to high-level competitions organized by national breed clubs. No cosmetic aids are allowed to improve a dog's appearance.

PREPARING FOR A SHOW

If you enter a show, you will need some basic equipment – a transportation crate, collar and lead, brush and comb, as well as bowls for food and water. Ensure that your Poodle is trimmed neatly, its teeth are tartar-free, its ears are clear of wax, and its nails clipped. Bathe your dog a few days before the show, so that its coat can develop a sheen from its natural oils.

Poodle's eyes are examined for size and colour

IN THE RING

In some countries, Toy and Miniature Poodles will first be measured at the shoulder to ensure that they conform to the national breed standard. When you are called into the ring, set your Poodle in its "show stance". Practise this at home using food rewards; these are also acceptable in the show ring. The judge examines your dog's body closely, running hands over its skin, feeling muscles and joints, and inspecting the mouth.

Owner holds dog, so that it can be examined by judge

THE JUDGE'S INSPECTION

After carefully inspecting all the dogs, the judge is likely to decide on a short list of six or seven. These dogs will then be examined once more, although the examination will not be as rigorous as the first. Remember, the judge is also assessing your dog's temperament – any nervousness or aggression will be noted.

ASSESSING MOVEMENT

After the judge has finished the physical examination, your Poodle's movement is evaluated. You will be asked to walk with your dog at a trot around the ring; if it is hesitant or awkward in its movement, it will be penalized. How you and your dog work together may also be assessed.

THE PRIZE-GIVING

Finally, the judge will award rosettes for first, second, and third places, and sometimes for the additional categories of "reserve" and "highly commended". If your dog's appearance does not conform to the specific criteria of the national breed standard, it will not win. However, bear in mind that this does not mean that it is in any way a second-rate dog.

COSTS OF SHOWING

Showing your Poodle does not have to be costly. If you show your own dog, your only expenses will be entry fees, transport, and accommodation. However, at the highest levels of the show circuit, professional trainers and handlers are sometimes employed. This can be very expensive, and there are few dogs that are so successful that their handling costs can be recouped through stud fees and puppy sales. If you decide that you are not interested in serious exhibiting and prize-winning, a far more sensible approach to showing your Poodle is to see it as a pleasurable hobby for you and your dog.

BREED STANDARD

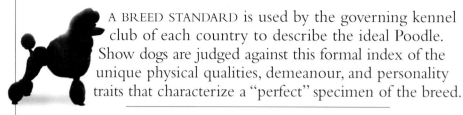

A BREED STANDARD is used by the governing kennel club of each country to describe the ideal Poodle. Show dogs are judged against this formal index of the unique physical qualities, demeanour, and personality traits that characterize a "perfect" specimen of the breed.

POODLE
UTILITY GROUP
(Last revised March 1994)

Reproduced by kind permission of
The Kennel Club
London, England

GENERAL APPEARANCE Well balanced, elegant looking with very proud carriage.

CHARACTERISTICS Distinguished by a special type of clip for show activity and by a type of coat which does not moult.

TEMPERAMENT Gay-spirited and good-tempered.

HEAD AND SKULL Long and fine with slight peak. Skull not broad, moderate stop. Foreface strong, well chiselled, not falling away under eyes; cheekbones and muscle flat. Lips tight-fitting. Chin well defined but not protruding. Head in proportion to size of dog.

EYES Almond-shaped, dark, not set too close together, full of fire and intelligence.

EARS Leathers long and wide, set low, hanging close to face.

MOUTH Jaws strong with perfect, regular complete scissor bite, i.e. upper teeth closely overlapping lower teeth and set square to the jaws. A full set of 42 teeth is desirable.

NECK Well proportioned, of good length and strong to admit of the head being carried high and with dignity. Skin fitting tightly at the throat.

FOREQUARTERS Well laid back shoulders, strong and muscular. Legs set straight from shoulders, well muscled.

BODY Chest deep and moderately wide. Ribs well sprung and rounded. Back short, strong, slightly hollowed; loins broad and muscular.

HINDQUARTERS Thighs well developed and muscular; well bent stifles, hocks well let down; hind legs turning neither in nor out.

FEET Tight, proportionately small, oval in shape, turning neither in nor out, toes arched, pads thick and hard, well cushioned. Pasterns strong.

TAIL Set on rather high, carried at slight angle away from body, never curled or carried over back, thick at root. Customarily docked.

GAIT/MOVEMENT Sound, free and light movement essential with plenty of drive.

COAT Very profuse and dense; of good harsh texture. All short hair close, thick and curly. It is strongly recommended that the traditional lion clip be adhered to.

COLOUR All solid colours. Whites and creams to have black nose, lips and eye rims, black toenails desirable. Browns to have dark amber eyes, dark liver nose, lips, eye rims and toenails. Apricots to have dark eyes with black points or deep amber eyes with liver points. Blacks, silvers and blues to have black nose, lips, eye rims and toenails. Creams, apricots, browns, silvers and blues may show varying shades of the same colour for up to 18 months. Clear colours preferred.

SIZE
Poodles (Standard) Over 38 cms (15 ins).
Poodles (Miniature) Height at shoulder should be under 38 cms (15 ins) but not under 28 cms (11ins).
Poodles (Toy) Height at shoulder should be under 28 cms (11 ins).

FAULTS Any departure from the foregoing points should be considered a fault and the seriousness with which the fault should be regarded should be in exact proportion to its degree.

NOTE Male animals should have two apparently normal testicles fully descended into the scrotum.

GLOSSARY

ABDOMEN Body cavity between chest and pelvis.
CROUP/RUMP The part of the back from the front of the pelvis to root of tail.
DENTITION The number and arrangement of teeth.
DEWCLAW Fifth digit on the inside of the legs.
DEWLAP Loose, pendulous skin under the throat.
ELBOW The joint between the upper arm and the forearm.
FOREARM The bone of forelegs, between elbow and wrist.
FOREQUARTERS Front part of dog, excluding head and neck.
GAIT The pattern of footsteps at various rates of speed, each pattern diagnosed by a particular rhythm and footfall.
HINDQUARTERS Rear part of dog from loin.
HOCK The tarsus or collection of bones of the hind leg forming the joint between the second thigh and the metatarsus.
KEEL Bone forming floor of chest (breastbone/sternum).

KNUCKLING OVER Faulty structure of carpus (wrist) joint causing it to double forward under weight of the dog.
LEATHER The flap of the ear.
LOIN Region of the body on either side of the vertebral column between the last ribs and the hindquarters.
OCCIPUT Upper, back point of skull.
PASTERN The region of the foreleg between the carpus, or wrist, and the digits.
PELVIS A framework of bones formed by the pelvic arch.
SKULL Bony regions of the head. Usually meant as section of head from stop to occiput.
STIFLE The joint of the hind leg between the thigh and the second thigh. The dog's knee.
STOP The step up from muzzle to skull; indentation between the eyes where the nasal bone and skull meet.
UPPER ARM The humerus, or bone of the foreleg, between the shoulder blade and the elbow.
WITHERS The highest point of the body, immediately behind the neck.

INDEX

ACKNOWLEDGMENTS

AUTHOR'S ACKNOWLEDGMENTS
Many thanks to Nic Kynaston, Stefan Morris, Karen O'Brien, Clare Driscoll, and their efficient DK production team, and to Patricia Holden White for convincing several Poodles to be positively obedient in Tracy Morgan's photography studio. Further thanks to Drs. Francis Barr and Sheila Crispin at the University of Bristol's Department of Clinical Medicine for clinical X-rays and photos of Poodle medical problems, Peter Kertesz for photographs of teeth and jaw conditions, Kathleen W. Rees and E. Anne Beswick for their experienced advice on breeding and showing, and to Amanda Hawthorne and Dr Ivan Berger at the Waltham Centre for Pet Nutrition for detailed advice on Poodle energy requirements. Finally, many thanks to all the members of the Poodle Club who completed questionnaires on Poodle behaviour.

PUBLISHER'S ACKNOWLEDGMENTS
Dorling Kindersley would like to thank photographer Tracy Morgan for her invaluable contribution to the book. Also special thanks to Tracy's photographic assistants: Sally Bergh-Roose and Stella Smyth-Carpenter. We are also grateful to Patricia Holden White for her advice and help on photographic sessions. Thanks to Jill Fornary, Cressida Joyce, Helen Thompson, and Sarah Wilde. Thanks also to Karin Woodruff for the index. Finally, we would like to thank the following people for lending their dogs and/or for modelling:

Pamela Alesworth and "Dakarta Digging For Gold"; Wendy Bartlet; Ben Brandstätter; Jayne Barber and "Amber" (Alpenden Summer Elegance); Stefanie Carpenter; Suzanne Collins; Roberto Costa; Giles Gale and "Melchie"; Angelo and Nina Ghiggini and "Pippa"; Mary Howarth and "Alfie" (Black Sentiment of Idadun); Lesley Howard; Jahel Kahla; Nic Kynaston; Sandra Martin, "Eddie", and the Philora Silver Cavender Puppies; Jan Mason and "Vinny" (Vinzent Aus Dem Schneckenhaus), "Jodie" (Braesterrie Monta Rosa Aprika), and "Bart"; Mr and Mrs Minette and "Max"; Franklyn Morris; Hector Morris; Stefan Morris; Karen O'Brien; Hannah Paynter, "Stevie" (Somanic White Willow), and Beau (Country Squire from Somanic); Mrs Rose Prince and "Lucy"; Gina Riley; Christine Properjohn and "PJ "; Jackie Stacy and Kymalaya Flame Kisted at Clarrich, Clarrich Moonlight Melody, Clarrich Fancy That, and Opella Moon Raker at Clarrich; Cindy Staples and

"Spankey"; Stella Smyth-Carpenter; Sarah Wilde; Mr and Mrs D. Withrington, "Toffee" (Taladayga on Parade with Suedor), and "Cleo" (Roushakas Express Wishes to Suedor).

PHOTOGRAPHIC CREDITS
Every effort has been made to trace the copyright holders, and we apologize in advance for any unintentional omissions. We would be pleased to insert the appropriate acknowledgments in any subsequent edition of this publication.

All photography by Tracy Morgan except:
AKG Photo: 68cr, 6cr;
Aquila Photo/Ulrike Schanz: 2, 9tr, 19tr;
Bridgeman Art Library/Southampton City Art Gallery: 69tl © ADAGP, Paris and DACS, London 1997, **Bonhaus, London:** 69tc, **Private Collection:** 66cr;
Christie's Images: 6bl;
Bruce Coleman Ltd./Uwe Walz: 6tl;
E.T. Archive: 69tr;
Mary Evans Picture Library: 68cl;
Giraudon/Musee D'Angers: 66cl;
Hulton Getty: 68bl;
Lauros-Giraudon, Musee de la Ville de Paris, Musee Carnavalet: 66br;
National Canine Defence League/Barry Plummer: 24tr;
Andrew Syred/Microscopix: 56c.

Key: l=left, r=right, t=top, c=centre, a=above, b=below

ILLUSTRATIONS
Andrew Beckett: 62–63;
Karen Cochrane: 49;
Samantha Elmhurst: 57, 59;
Jane Pickering: 39.